Parenting
in the
Age of
Anxiety

Parenting
in the
Age of
Anxiety

RAISING CHILDREN IN INDIA IN THE 21st CENTURY

ABHA ADAMS

ALEPH

ALEPH BOOK COMPANY
An independent publishing firm
promoted by *Rupa Publications India*

First published in India in 2022
by Aleph Book Company
7/16 Ansari Road, Daryaganj
New Delhi 110 002

ISBN: 978-93-91047-81-8

1 3 5 7 9 10 8 6 4 2

Printed in India

CONTENTS

INTRODUCTION

When I was invited to write a book on the current challenges of parenting, my first thought was: do we really need yet another self-help book on this? Shelves in bookshops appear to be heaving with 'How To' guide books on every topic ranging from keeping pet fish to parenting. The first ever book on parenting was authored by the American paediatrician Dr Benjamin Spock in 1946. *The Common Sense Book of Baby and Child Care* sold 50 million copies and became one of the bestselling books of the twentieth century. I know it wasn't on my parents' bookshelf, so clearly they didn't feel the need to seek his help, and my grandparents definitely didn't refer to any literature when they were bringing up my parents. So why is it that parents today feel the need for guidance and support from a variety of sources? I thought back to my struggles as a parent and an educator. When my son hit his teens and I was floundering, my helpline was the author Haim Ginott. His books, *Between Parent & Teenager* and *Teacher & Child*, helped me gain an understanding of what my son was going through, and how I could help him and come to terms with it myself. Over the last three decades as an educator, I drew on these texts extensively in my conversations with parents and children, but looking back, I feel the last decade has been the hardest so far for parents, children, and educators alike.

Over the course of writing this book, I reflected on the last decade, both as an educator and as a parent, and the strands of change began to weave themselves into a pattern of what I now see have been cataclysmic shifts in our society. What are the changes we are experiencing, in families, in our support structures, in the way we live, in the way schools operate, and in the way we teach? What are the pressures we are battling against? While living and working through various crises, we don't fully understand the adaptations we are forced to make; it is only in hindsight, when we look back with an objective perspective, that we see the pulls and tugs of the times we lived through and how they changed us and our lives. These shifts have impacted us as parents and teachers, and significantly changed the futures of our children. I hoped that by writing this book I would be able to, in a small way, record the voices of this community that raises children. And record their efforts as they combat the combined forces of commercialization, digitalization, and a worldwide uncertainty regarding these complex and changing times. Let's face it, insecurity over the future clouds our horizon and I sometimes yearn for the certainties that previous generations may have had.

So this book is about the journey, of parents, children, and educators as they travel together, for the fourteen years of schooling and beyond. The first chapter looks at new parents and young children; the second at the tween years (between the ages of eight and twelve); and the third delves into the world of teenagers. The fourth chapter walks with children with special needs and their parents and caregivers. The fifth chapter explores mental health—a topic that has become hugely important. I wanted the book to reflect the voices of all of us who contribute to raising children. Clearly, it takes more than the proverbial village to raise a child. Other than family, nuclear and extended, now it takes a community of educators, counsellors, and therapists.

Writing this book helped me understand my own responses to raising children—both as a mother and an educator. Parenting starts with the life-altering experience of holding one's newborn child, seeing her take her first few steps, and then walking her to school, her hand in yours. It progresses to the turbulent years of growing up and adolescence, when she grows, discovers herself, and steps into the world. In truth, parenting never really ceases, because our children will always be just that—our children. As parents, we hopefully forge nurturing relationships with them as young adults; our desire to always protect them from the pain, disappointment, and loss that they will experience is something we can't control and that is a hard lesson for us to learn. It certainly was one of the hardest I learnt.

Every individual has her story, and our children will eventually write their own narratives, with all the ups and downs that life inevitably has in store for all of us. With this in mind, I decided my starting point would be conversations with parents, children, and educators about the pressures they felt at various points in their journey. And as the conversations began, some individual, some in focused group discussions, the pain points began to emerge with remarkable clarity. Over the eighteen months of speaking to individuals and groups, the challenges everyone seemed to be wrestling with reflect our changing times and the fractured sense of reality that we are all coping with.

I am reminded of a generational gap here, while using the word 'cope'. My mother spent a year with me in the UK in 1985, helping us raise our son. She was surrounded by our friends, mostly in their late thirties, who often spoke to her about not being able to 'cope' and how depressed they felt. My mother, who had experienced Partition, World War II, had been a refugee, and worked her way up in life just couldn't comprehend *why* my friends couldn't cope! 'What is this word—cope?' she would ask me with increasing irritation. 'Why can't they just get on with living? They have too much of everything—that's their problem!'

Maybe that is our problem. Young parents today seem to be at a crossroads when it comes to what they want for their children. It is not an intuitive and instinctive response to parenting, like it was for my grandparents and parents. In fact, it is being guided by consumer-driven industries. Parents are faced with a proliferation of attractive products, enticing guarantees, and specialist advice. It is a successful marketing onslaught, and one to which they find themselves succumbing. In the last decade, our society has become intensely consumer driven—we have industries around parenting ranging from how to prepare for the birth to which prestigious school and coaching classes your toddler should go to—all kinds of products to build your baby into a veritable genius adept at multifarious activities from language acquisition to sports, music, dance, chess, golf, etc. Confronted by this bewildering array of promises, we lose our way.

This decision-making builds up enormous pressures on young parents. They want to do the best for their child, of course, but how does one decide what is the best course? Should she be doing more than one activity a day? How much screen time is okay? How can we keep up with theme-based birthday parties or indeed afford the kind of return gifts that she received? For affluent parents, these may not be burning questions, but middle-class parents struggle, as do those who are just about making ends meet. Because, after all, children across the board desire everything that tinsel town has to offer.

This has been compounded by the phenomenon of advancing adolescence—a term I often use to explain to educators and parents how every generation of students entering nursery school appear to be smarter, sharper, and faster at growing up. Parents and teachers are dismayed by this generation's precociousness, and flash points with students we used to experience in the eleventh or twelfth grade are now reflected in students between the sixth and eighth grade. I look at this phenomenon of Kids Growing Older Younger Faster (KGOYF), an acronym coined by a talented marketing specialist no doubt, in the second chapter. Children are faced with the challenges of early puberty, and struggle to understand what's happening to their bodies and emotions. Meanwhile parents are floundering, wondering how they can approach the 'talk' about menstruation, and schools are flummoxed by whether they should be holding 'growing up' sessions for their eight-year-old students. What a polite phrase that is—'growing up' workshops. Not adolescent education, and heavens forbid, not sex education.

I took a particularly deep dive into the pain points of the thirteen to eighteen years age group in the third chapter. Middle school brings in its wake a host of hurdles for parents and children and, needless to say, educators and schools as well. Primary school seems to be one long halcyon summer compared to the head on collision with adolescence. It is a stage when hormones are jumping, academic and social pressures are mounting, and a turbo-charged rebellious being finds herself at a crossroads almost beyond childhood and yet nowhere near adulthood. Parents are confused, and educators are engaged in firefighting for most of the school day. Surely, there have always been teenagers. I was one once, as was my mother before me. I rebelled all the time, and on each occasion my mother sanguinely denied ever going against her parents' wishes. Each time, I would remind her that she spent her youth chucking stones at British soldiers, joining marches for the Congress, burning her clothes, and wearing khadi, and eventually running away to marry my father—everything that her parents disapproved of. So what has changed now when it comes to teenage rebellion, when they desert parents for friends and believe they are adults? I believe parental expectations, which are at an all-time high, are the reason we feel it more keenly than before. We believe that as parents we need to inhabit a perfect world with perfect children, and that makes accepting our teen's adolescence much more difficult.

Which is why the revelations of some neuroscientists on how the teen mind works was so reassuring. It explained why they are impossible to live with and to teach, and definitely impossible to get through to. It made me think deeply about my own rebellious years when I believed that my friends and I were always right, and my parents and teachers were, of course, always wrong. There are some generational gaps that will always remain no matter which century we are referring to.

Whatever our dilemmas, as parents we are always ambitious for our children and, with the best of intentions, we tend to heap our expectations on them. Competitive parenting also raises its ugly head when we begin comparing our children with other children. This leads to a breakdown in the relationship between parents and children. As academic pressure ratchets up in middle school, we begin to see a split between the teenager and the adults in their lives. This breakdown raises the levels of stress and anxiety in our teens as well as a great deal of fear, primarily, a fear of failure. Along with this fear comes a deep sense of not being good enough in their parents' eyes, as well as their own.

This came through time and time again in the narratives of students who experienced anxiety that led to panic attacks, depression, and self-harm in many cases. What hit me was the scale of the mental health crisis we are facing, in schools, and in our homes. The two years of lockdown, isolation, and uncertainty due to the Covid-19 pandemic has worsened this. And yet, it is a reality that is being brushed under the carpet by institutions and, in many cases, by our denial as parents. Why is that so? Why are we avoiding talking about the mental health concerns of our children? Today our children are facing a mental health crisis like never before, which is in part being fuelled by the accelerated digitalization of our lives.

I believe this digital takeover—and by that I mean the increasing addiction to screens—is taking time away from all of us, preventing us from connecting as family and friends, and consequently proving detrimental to the critical art of conversation and dialogue. This lack of communication inevitably leads to cracks in relationships within the family unit and, for educators, reflects in our relationships with our students. Our teens spend up to six hours a day on their phones alone—where does that leave any time for talking to families? We see this phenomenon wherever we go, with infants in strollers holding smartphones, families in restaurants where all members are looking down at their devices, on buses, on trains, in markets, in cars, even in a cinema hall, or a theatre while watching a play—humanity is looking down at their screens.

I used the word addiction earlier and there is enough research around what causes this obsessive relationship with our smartphones. It is being treated by doctors as Screen Dependency Disorder (SDD), a condition that needs medical intervention. With the advent of social media platforms such as Facebook (only for oldies now I'm informed), and more significantly Instagram, Snapchat, YouTube, and Twitter, teens are constantly hooked to their mind-altering and numbing phone screens.

'We're living by proxy', a student ruefully remarked. She spends her days at home scrolling through her Instagram account, being a voyeur. In a nutshell, teens today live their lives not just following, but aching to be the bold and beautiful influencers who have perfect bodies and perfect lives, with clothes to die for, holidays in exotic locations, parties that are the stuff of legend, and happily-ever-after endings. This is the ephemeral stencil they try and build their lives around. Chasing this invented and Photoshopped mirage leads to deep disappointment and the feeling of not being good enough, quickly followed by depression and despair.

Critically, the natural process of growing up and developing a sense of who they are, an understanding of their beliefs, and the shaping of their almost adult self doesn't occur when it should. It gets sidetracked, distracted, and confused by the different messaging our adolescents receive from social media. It is at this time that both parents and educators need to be truly invested in understanding, supporting, and communicating with them. It's a tough call, because they reject us at this stage, but as adults we have to give them the space as well as the buttress of family and friends that they need.

When it comes to parenting, it is never a case of one size fits all. Parenting is learnt behaviour and we find ourselves replaying the way we were parented as children in some cases. It is impossible to find a rule book that teaches you to be a good parent. It is hard, bewildering, and most of us tend to beat ourselves up about it. I was constantly beset by my 'failures' as I saw it. What I did learn over time was to be kinder to myself and accept that parents make mistakes. The myth of happy families and ideal children and perfect parents is just that, a myth. What I also learned through this journey was that parenting is a work in progress, and our expectations of ourselves and our children need to be raised or lowered according to the circumstances. That, as a parent, I can never give up on the process.

However, I find young parents are uncertain about how they want to raise their children. Parenting advice is coming to them from all quarters. From print and electronic media, webinars, websites, and specialist life coaches (now there's a new term!). Living in nuclear family set-ups, young parents don't have access to help and support from their own extended families. In many cases they feel that their words of wisdom are outdated and therefore seek out specialists to help raise their children. The advice they receive may be good but it also pulls them in different directions, and making the right decision becomes both difficult and frustrating. This also results in anxious parenting which is reflected in anxious children. Have we begun, in a sense, to 'outsource' parenting instead of forging some fundamental and original approaches?

The journey of parents of differently-abled children is not just complex but both poignant and challenging. This book would be incomplete without their voice, which captures their determination, courage, and above all, their unstinting efforts in securing the rights of their children from the community and society at large.

According to the 2011 Census, India has 26.8 million persons with special needs. The UNESCO report '2019 State of Education Report of India: Children with Disabilities' reveals that there are 7,864,636 children with disabilities in India which is 1.7 per cent of the total child population. Further, three-fourths of the children aged five and one-fourth of children between the ages of five and nineteen don't attend schools in India, and there is a surge in the number of dropouts with each successive level of schooling.

Are we denying our children their basic fundamental rights? It appears we are. Parents spoke candidly about the unimaginable pressures of getting the right medical advice, securing educational opportunities, and the distressing lack of support from society and government. Their narratives speak for themselves; for me the hope lies in the contributions of individuals and institutions, both within schools and industry, who are taking significant steps to address this inequity.

And what of the future? What lies ahead for our young as they navigate through these unpredictable and insecure times? The last few years of the pandemic have deepened the uncertainties we had come to expect of the future. There had been considerable drum beating around the need for twenty-first-century skills to prepare our children for an unknown world in terms of work. Attributed to the projected acceleration of automation and Artificial Intelligence in industries, job losses were predicted and that in itself was causing a churn in education and in children's prospects. The pandemic, successive global shutdowns, and the possibility of recession have raised the question of whether we can predict anything at all about what lies ahead.

When you think about it, our children have faced unprecedented times of trauma and loss. The mental health situation, which was already precarious, has worsened significantly. Confusion, stress, and fear have eroded their sense of what they can possibly expect in a future that changes shape every passing day. The hardest hit have always been the poor, particularly women and children, and it is no different in this instance. Early research by the UN in 2020 highlighted the adversity, disenfranchisement, hunger, violence, and abuse experienced by women. The following year, a World Economic Forum report included a reference to a study conducted in India by BMJ Paediatrics that reported the escalation of violence and abuse in homes.[1]

And yet in my conversations with students living through the heightened trauma of the last few years, I was struck by their strength and resilience in the face of various obstacles. And it is this singular observation that gave me hope about the future. As lives hit the pause button, some went under with depression and anxiety, and are still finding their way back. Many others recognized that what had held them together was the love and support they received from family and friends. They took stock of their young lives, something which

---

[1]Amira Ghouaibi, 'The Pandemic Has Hurt Women's Health. This is why it is bad for everyone', World Economic Forum, accessed on 1 August 2022.

many adults have been unable to do! They reflected on what was meaningful to them, and realized that, eventually, the only thing that gave meaning to life was the warmth of the relationships they had, and the love they gave and received. This is a life lesson that many of us adults have never fully embraced. The virtual perfection projected at them was suspended.

Instead, their focus became helping each other, and extending that help to the larger community. They were mindful about what gave them joy and sought to be in the present moment. They saw the fallacy of believing that, as a species at the top of the food chain, we were in control of our lives, of nature, and of our world. Underlying their words were compassion, humility, and a genuine commitment to making our world a safe environment.

I have hope, and I have faith that a future that I may not see is safe in the hands of our children.

1

PARENTING IS FOR LIFE

The first time ever I saw your face
I thought the sun rose in your eyes
and the moon and the stars
were the gifts you gave
to the dark, and the endless skies
my love
to the dark, and the endless skies.

—Ewan MacColl, 1957

Nothing quite prepares you for the moment when you first hold your newborn child. It was 1984 and a freezing winter in Leeds, United Kingdom. After twenty-eight hours in labour, I was struggling with childbirth. I remember my husband, Bill, holding my hand urging me to hang in there, my mother praying from our home since she could not bear to hear my pain, and the wonderful midwives who helped me find the strength to avoid a caesarean delivery. I had almost given up when my son finally decided to greet the world. The hospital staff had brought an emergency incubator and were ready for the worst. I can remember how, before I collapsed with exhaustion, I heard his first cry and my only question was—is the baby okay? Does he have fingers and toes? It's a healthy baby boy, they assured me, and whisked him away while I passed out.

Holding him for the first time, seeing and feeling the life you have held within you—nothing prepares you for the journey this soul

1

is going to take with you. Nothing prepares you for your journey as a parent, the mistakes you will make, the commitment and love parenting requires, and the fears and demons you will battle along the way. Even in my weakened state I can remember the emotions of fierce protection. That stays with you. You want to keep this being safe and loved and free from pain and suffering. And here's the thing—over the years life teaches you that it's not possible to do that. One can love unconditionally, but to imagine that we can control their circumstances in the future is madness. But for several years I was and to some extent, still am, afflicted with this madness.

For the danger is that we begin to believe that this is my child, in many respects an extension of me. It leads us to foist expectations, aspirations, and our unfulfilled dreams on their unwritten pages of life at such an early age. Then, when disappointment sets in—when they cannot live up to the image you have developed, all the disappointment and pain become personal, and that is a terrible wrench.

Your children are not your children.
They are the sons and daughters of life's longing for itself.
They come through you but not from you,
and though they are with you, yet they belong not to you.
You may give them your love but not your thoughts
for they have their own thoughts.
You may house their bodies but not their souls
for their souls dwell in the house of tomorrow,
which you cannot visit, not even in your dreams.

—Kahlil Gibran

I was curious to understand this life changing moment for parents, because, let's face it, nothing is ever the same after you hold your newly born child. And sure enough the parents I spoke to, particularly the fathers, found it hard to put in words what they felt at that moment.

Raghu was the first to hold his baby daughter. 'Because her birth was so complicated, Amna (his daughter) was taken immediately to an ICU for babies so none of us could see her, but I found my way there and got to hold her. She immediately opened her eyes and looked at me. It was an amazing feeling. Too many feelings went through my mind, there are no words to describe it. First there was relief, and then unconditional love. I felt no matter what, I have to protect her. And it has changed me, since then I function in a more responsible way.'

The responsibility hits home almost immediately! When Bhanu first held her son—'There were just so many emotions at that time. There was happiness, fear, stress; my hormones were all over the place. He was so tiny. I've never seen such a tiny human in my life, I've never held a baby. And you can't even hear them breathe, I just kept checking whether he was okay. And the responsibility for another human being just hits you.'

Who would have predicted that three years later, the experience of giving birth in 2020, during the pandemic, would be so very different and traumatic. Ishara's daughter Samina was born on 12 June in New York. The city locked down in March 2020, when they were at the epicentre of the pandemic, and by April she felt it was the worst place to be in the world.

'I was very fearful, we tried not to get sick and were extremely careful. I was nervous about going into labour, and we didn't know if hospital beds would be available. Many women I knew moved out of the city, and rented homes, so that they could give birth at home because hospitals would be overrun. Partners were not allowed to be with the mother. I had a birth plan which seems so ridiculous now, because there was no certainty about anything.'

She gave birth in a mask, and because her amniotic fluid was dangerously low and the baby was in distress, she was rushed in for a caesarean section. Locked in a room for three days with masks 24/7, the loneliness was terrifying. All parents struggle in the first few months and I was fortunate to have my mother by my side, but Ishara was alone and figuring out breastfeeding by watching YouTube videos! We all remember the lack of sleep, but the endless fatigue was offset by the presence of family and friends who would troop in to meet the baby and you. Sadly for Ishara, there was only isolation during a hard winter. Family couldn't travel to see the baby and friends could not visit and she tearfully recounted her despair—'I felt so alone. I felt this lack of touch...not getting hugged....'

PREPARING FOR THE BABY

Preparing for the arrival of a newborn is so different for every individual. My son was not planned, I had just landed a new job with the BBC and I was terrified. England was still unfamiliar territory and in brief, I was beside myself. What did I do? Turned to my mother, of course, who promised to come and stay and raise my child. I know that for my mother pregnancy was a matter of fact, a part of life, and life went on. In her case, as a school principal, she had gone to school until a few hours before she had me. I was lucky that the BBC's equal opportunities policy did not allow them to discriminate and I landed my dream job without having to compromise.

The 1980s were the start of parenting as an industry in the UK, and yes, there were innumerable books, magazines, and workshops available for would-be parents. It was also the time of new-age birthing with sessions available on giving birth at home, painting your walls a certain colour to quell an anxious foetus, giving birth in water, etc. The more I read, the more anxious I got, imagining the worst that could happen. I joined a group of would-be moms who urged me to consider a natural birth at home. I guess they saw me as an exotic representative of ancient and traditional cultures and half hoped I would opt for birthing by holding on to a tree. I had my fill of new-age birthing when they exchanged anecdotes of burying the placenta in their gardens, and worse still, frying the placenta and eating it as a ritual. I never went back to the group. I never attended any antenatal Lamaze classes either, what had worked for my mother I thought, would work for me, which was basically—get on with your life.

Experiences vary. Raghu and his wife, Fiona, read a lot. 'We went for Lamaze classes, but Fiona forgot everything once childbirth started,' Raghu said. 'For me, I learnt how to help during her hormonal changes and various stages of the pregnancy. I learnt to give her whatever she wanted and to help her during labour.'

For Bhanu, her son was a surprise baby. 'When I heard I was pregnant, I was shocked, really really shocked. I didn't believe it would happen so quickly. I wasn't mentally or physically prepared for the journey and it took me a month and a half to digest it. And every day I would wonder, can I do it? How will I do it? We didn't prepare for parenting. We joined no support groups, did not go to Lamaze classes, didn't read books, we lived a normal life. I had a good pregnancy, I worked, built a nursery which kept me busy for months, and finished it ten days before Aman was born.'

Understandably, younger parents like Udit feel that the experiences and advice offered by the older generation is just not valid any more. 'There is such a massive difference in the times when our parents had us; we are now almost thirty-five, so a lot of the information they passed on doesn't apply to us as parents in a nuclear family. The older generation had the privilege of many relatives chipping in, in various ways, but today we don't have that. I am fearful now, I didn't feel fearful before, but now I have so much more to lose. You become a little timid after having a child. I was bold earlier.'

EXPECTATIONS, ASPIRATIONS, OVER-PROGRAMMING

For parents, expectations and aspirations set in early. At the same time, the values and the behaviours the child will learn and display are also forged very early. The baby watches you, senses the energies that surround the home, and attunes to the atmosphere around him. Do parents develop an approach to these early years? Do we consciously set about inculcating values in our little children?

Samina had her daughter after an intense IVF process. She shared that, as a couple, they were 'just teaching her to be humble, compassionate, and empathetic to those less fortunate', and believed that values like respect for the elders would automatically follow suit.

But how do you, as a parent, acquire these values? And sure enough, as Samina points out, it's what we learn from our parents—it's learnt behaviour. 'I've always known a joint family. My father had six brothers and sisters and my mother seven sisters! It's quite a jamboree. So I never grew up alone, I always had cousins with me. The house was always open. My parents had very strong relationships with our neighbours, and they were particularly close to the landlord that we stayed with for a very long time. My mother got pregnant after eleven years; my father had to go to UK, he was a metallurgical engineer, and our landlord whom we called dadaji looked after my mother, who could not travel, right up to the point I was born. They were very compassionate to everyone, so I learnt from them and we want to do the same.'

And as parents we strive to shape these early years. At the age of forty-one, Samina took the decision to quit her full-time job after she became a mother because, unlike the joint family she grew up in, they were now a nuclear family without supportive grandparents to help.

'We thought my being at home would give my daughter a sense of security. We tried to do things that she would pick up by example. So we both began learning the piano, it is something we are really struggling with, but we are trying our best so that she hears the piano, and actually enjoys it. There are three things that we're fond of—books, music, and swimming. If these become a part of your life at an early age, it sees a child through. The other thing we consciously do is not watch TV. So we stopped watching TV ever since she was born. We only watch the news once in a while to see the election results.'

I thought about my own value system and how had I internalized what I saw around me as a child. I can remember that hard work was a family ethic. Both my parents worked. My father was a banker, my mum a leading educationist, and post Partition they worked ceaselessly to support an extended family, getting brothers and sisters educated, married, and setting them up in their homes. True, it was a patriarchal unit, with my father as an authoritative and a somewhat autocratic head. And he and I would clash incessantly in my teens. But what I did absorb was the kindness I saw around me. In the joint family I grew up in—which provided a support system—all my aunts and uncles worked, and so the principle of hard work and effort always stayed central to my being.

Clearly, my son saw this and I remember the first few sentences he wrote when he was six, about his family and the experience of moving to India, in these words. 'My nani works very hard and is very kind. She picks me up from my bus every day. My mother is very kind and cares and works very hard. My father is a happy person.' A telling tale and you can make of that what you will. All through his teenage years I struggled with his rejection of the ethic of hard work which he only rediscovered in his thirties.

Udit's goal for his son is that he should be happy—'Because when you're happy from within you can give happiness outside. If you have inner peace and good values, you will have a far better life than chasing ambitions and goals. Life has become so fast moving that we are benchmarking happiness with things you buy with money, and eventually you realize that will not bring happiness.'

Raghu and Fiona want Amna to be 'a good person, adaptable, be sensible, be wise, and be helpful'. They add, 'We have no dreams about what she wants to do in life. We will support her, make sure she gives her best, and does it right. For us the most important thing is that she is a happy, healthy kid. The greatest challenge is the pollution and the environment. We're scared about what the world will be like in twenty years for her. We are mindful of enjoying each day as it is and we will do our best to ensure she is prepared.'

And yet, no matter how hard we try as parents, our aspirations and expectations are irrepressible, and there is the unshakeable belief that my child has to be a genius—learning languages, doing every new-fangled activity. We're over-programming our children's lives and have fuelled an industry of active kids and their mommies. And this sector has been quick to piggy back on the online opportunities available for aspirational parents during the pandemic.

WhatsApp mom groups are buzzing with questions about what is available. 'I was constantly being asked by other mums if I am subscribing to Music Together music classes,' says Samina, wearily. Prior to the pandemic, she came across mothers who were taking their toddlers to two preschools on different days. Why? To learn Japanese and German. The children must have been twenty-two months old and were already busy six days a week. Samina began to feel the pressure to do the same.

'I felt immense pressure. I thought I had to keep pace with it, and I was fearful that my daughter was lagging behind and not doing things she should. Even summer holidays are planned so that children learn something. I haven't done anything like that with her, I let her swim, play on the beach. I feel pressured about whether I am doing the right thing? Is she learning?'

Why do our children have to be learning all the time? I was once asked for my advice at a parent session which compounded this almost desperate over-scheduling of children's time. The child was five years old, and besides attending kindergarten, she had Kumon mathematics, art and craft, and music and storytelling as activities through the week. 'Should I enrol her in Mandarin classes?' this anxious parent asked me. My baffled expression must have led her to justify this. 'She should be learning an international language and I thought Mandarin was the future, and that would be so useful to her in her college application?' I'm usually not lost for words, but on this occasion, words failed me.

Kiran Tara Singh, who has run her own successful preschool, is emphatic that the activities industry is a money-spinner. 'You're spending up to ₹800 an hour to get your child running through the plastic tunnels and playing amidst plastic balls. It's all indoors with hardly any light. They are throwing things all over the place, and my goodness, kids can be rough. They were shooting things; we never gave toy guns to children. Today, they're talking about guns, pointing it at you, and shooting. And they're playing shooting games on their video game sets; it's all coming from the digital software that we are giving them.'

This is a far cry from a childhood in the 1950s and 1960s, Peter Gray, the author of *Free to Learn* (2013), describes his childhood and the two educations he received during that time.

'We had school (which was not the big deal it is today), and we also had what I call a hunter-gatherer education. We played in mixed-age neighbourhood groups almost every day after school, often until dark. We played all weekend and all summer long. We had time to explore in all sorts of ways, and also time to become bored and figure out how to overcome boredom, time to get into trouble and find our way out of it, time to daydream, time to immerse ourselves in hobbies, and time to read comics and whatever else we wanted to read rather than the books assigned to us. What I learnt in my hunter-gatherer education has been far more valuable to my adult life than what I learnt in school, and I think others in my age group would say the same if they took time to think about it.'[1]

Around the world, psychologists, doctors, and educators are concerned about the reduction in playtime that has happened over the last ten years. In the US, children are so over scheduled that doctors are beginning to prescribe play.

A clinical report published in the September 2018 issue of *Pediatrics*, a journal by the American Academy of Pediatrics, provides necessary clarity and insight on the power of playtime for children. According to the report, 'Play is brain building for babies and young children'[2].

'For example, Circle Time in preschool is not about learning the alphabet or mastering Old MacDonald as much as it is learning to be part of a group, mastering the art of taking turns, and starting

[1]Peter Gray, 'The play deficit', *Aeon*, 18 September 2018.
[2]Michael Yogman, Andrew Garner, Jeffrey Hutchinson, Kathy Hirsh-Pasek, Roberta Michnick Golinkoff, 'The Power of Play: A Pediatric Role in Enhancing Development in Young Children', Pediatrics, September 2018.

to listen. Playing—unstructured time, with rules set by the kids (no adults acting as referee)—is how kids learn independence, problem-solving, social cues, and bravery. Now, parents jump in to solve the playground kerfuffle, spot with eagle eyes the dangers of tall trees and steep hills, and fail to let kids have any independence for fear that they will be abducted or hit by a car.'[3]

By denying them these avenues we are handing them over to assisted technology and screen time, both of which denote the beginning of a relationship where the controls lie firmly in the hands of Artificial Intelligence.

Sonya Philips, founder of Learning Matters, has started to 'educate' parents about this vital issue. She refers to *Teacher Tom's First Book*—'He talks about play and how it has all the cognitive ingredients in it. By play we don't mean going for tennis or lessons. Play is self-initiated, which you and I did as children. We were playing, using our imagination, making up the rules. So what was our brain doing when we were playing? We were initiating, that is a cognitive skill. Today, children don't know it, they are bored, they don't know what to do. Play allows for that part of the brain to grow.'

She is right. We learnt planning, execution, and that critical twenty-first-century skill we're focusing on these days—collaboration—all through play. Philips draws attention to all the cognitive skills children lack today because we deny them free play. This has led to what is being called 'executive function dysfunction'.

'These are all executive skills, it has nothing to do with intelligence. You can be super intelligent but you're not succeeding because you don't have executive skills. You don't know how to manage time; when do you do your homework, how do you plan—play is when all of this develops naturally.'

Clearly, parents and educators have not been able to sufficiently grasp what children stand to lose when they are deprived of play. Children lose the opportunity of acquiring this important cognitive

---

[3]Jenny Anderson, 'Why are our kids so miserable?', *Quartz*, 21 March 2016.

process that should come naturally in a playground. We take away their childhoods and prescribe in its stead a regimen of uniforms, backpacks, and passive instruction in a classroom with doors and windows shut to the world.

Kiran faces the same challenges in educating parents about the need for play, spending time outdoors, and doing a little bit of gardening. 'Children never really feel the heat. We have all played outdoors as children and loved it. That's when they learn to get messy in the mud, roll around the grass, and do fun things. So where has all the fun gone? I think all the fun has gone out of schooling. Children are coming into preschool more absorbed about what they have—my father's given me this, my father's given me that. The digital world has changed the conversation, where we are talking more about things; in many ways it's taken away the human angle. Where you earlier wanted to hold hands with your friend, you're no longer doing that any more because you're glued to a screen most of the time.'

And play needs to be unstructured—no play dates, but just play, with whatever they have, by themselves or with their friends. This down time, giving them space, and letting them be is critical. We are in danger of over-programming our children's lives to the extent that our children face a deficit of free time. We don't need to fill them to the brim with experiences. They need to be encouraged to make their own efforts, make their own mistakes, they have to exercise their own agency. Encourage activities that take time to master—learning a musical instrument, engaging in contact sport. Catch them being curious, encourage them to play outdoors, teach them to engage with their environment, and revel in the wonder of it all.

All of this came to a screeching halt during the Covid-19 pandemic. Astha's daughter started crawling the week lockdown started and walking in July, when outdoor play was the hardest hit.

'We were physically housebound, and we live in a flat, so I researched and bought a balancing ball, an inflatable swimming pool. I made sure she was doing a lot of sensory bins, so that she could experience different textures, and looking at birds from our balcony.

Then I started taking her out at 6.30 a.m. I felt beyond a point, the outdoors experience couldn't be replicated at home, so we started going to the playground two, three months ago—it was very challenging.'

PARENTING PRESSURE POINTS IN THE EARLY YEARS

As a working mother for all of my life, I have carried a sense of guilt. I have feared that I have missed out on my child's growing years, and blamed myself when things went wrong, and in hindsight, over-compensated. I can remember vividly my frequent but necessary travel to London when my son was three years old. He knew I was going to be away for a day or two, the overnight bag, which was ready and waiting for me, was the first indicator for him and I would wait fearfully for his reaction. True to form, every single time the taxi drew up outside the house and I bent down to hug him goodbye, he would tearfully hold on to me, 'Don't go, Mummy, please don't go.' I could feel the gut-wrenching upheaval in the pit of my stomach every time I reassured him I would be back and handed him to his father. Bill would share with me later that barely had the taxi turned the corner, than his tears had dried and he was leaping about playfully, looking forward to what Mummy would get him from London. But for me, the two and half hours on the train to London were journeys of guilt and tears and the 'if only' I could find a job where I did not have to travel refrain.

Looking back to the 1980s, I realize that as a parent I had it relatively easy. Today, parenting pressures are complex and unique. In our digital consumer-driven society, raising children appears to be beset with so many tough decisions that I have found parents floundering. Add to this the various industries that have grown around babies, children, and parents—no wonder there is confusion amongst our young parents about which road to take and what choices to make.

Take the baby industry for a start. I remember my mother telling me that when she was rushed to the hospital after coming home from work, she called my father and told him to come at once with the essentials—a basin, a towel, and a hairbrush. When it was my turn to do the same we got the same essential basics. Sure, Mothercare was around, but we were able to bypass that thanks to the tradition of hand-me-downs amongst our family and friends. We inherited baby clothes, a stroller, mats, and basins, and that just pretty much left the nappies for us to buy. In turn, once my son outgrew all the stuff, it was time to pack them off to whoever was having a baby next!

Today, baby care is out of control. Dr Shelja Sen, co-founder of the Children First Institute of Child & Adolescent Mental Health, writes about how the booming baby industry is exploiting gullible parents. 'No wonder we start filling up our homes with all the exorbitantly priced equipment, enrolling them in trending baby workshops (starting at two months), decorating nurseries with colour-coded accessories, hiring English-speaking nannies, and strutting them around in luxury labels. Not to mention the "must have" toys which "foster brain development" and "build cognitive skills"! Which parent can say no to those? If it is best for our kids and will give them a head start, then we are going to get it. No matter how…. Except that it is not. Whatever the baby industry might try to sell you, babies do not need or care for any of that stuff. All it does is create more stress and anxiety in parents of not doing enough for their babies. What we need is less "doing" and more of "being".'[4]

There was a time when it was not considered propitious to buy clothes and baby stuff in advance. Now I know of mothers-in-law who are packed off overseas to and come back with everything that is available in the booming baby industry.

Samina came across it too. 'We had to hire a nurse because I needed the care. And she came and said, "Where is the changing cot? Where is the diaper station?"—I laughed—a diaper station! And so I told my husband to rush off and buy it all. My husband calmly

---

[4]Shelja Sen, 'Babies need attuned mothers to form trusting bonds, not "experts"', *Indian Express*, 4 May 2019.

told me to relax, "We'll just change her on the bed, it worked for us, it will work for our daughter".'

And before you know it, it's time for preschool and that's another pressure point.

There was a time when it was hard to find a good school in the vicinity for children. Now, even preschools, which are seen as necessary experiences prior to regular school, are seeing long waiting lists, even as preschools continue to proliferate in every neighbourhood. It is an unregulated sector and the fees can range from ₹50,000 per annum to over ₹200,000 per annum.

Many schools are trying to convince parents that they will make their child 'school-ready'. Which means, in some cases, that a two-year-old is expected to colour and draw, identify the alphabet, attend workshops on communication, and recite poems barely out of nappies. Schools offer 'experiences' to eighteen-month-old babies in the form of a series of 'parenting experiences' with toddlers and reams of literature, as well as advice, from digital platforms and face to face workshops with expert trainers in this area.

This is a pet peeve of mine. Research and wisdom has proven time and time again that children should start formal learning at six years of age. The Scandinavian countries we are rushing off to emulate start school at seven in most cases, while we have a burgeoning industry that begins to put pressure on children and parents from the time they are eighteen months old. There are Android-based apps that help mothers lose the pregnancy fat, figure out what to feed their baby and themselves; guides to visiting new mums and their babies, and gifting ideas for baby showers—now there's a social custom our ever eager consumerist society has embraced with gusto.

But back to the world of preschools, which can be a daunting experience unless you are prepared to throw yourself headlong into the very new culture of the very young parent. Sabina shares the bias she faced when her daughter started preschool. 'We were told quite bluntly that we would be the odd ones out because we were forty-one when she went to nursery, whereas the rest of the crowd was about twenty-nine years old. So there was a huge age gap. I was the only one who was working, in the middle of a career, whereas the rest were younger, married, and rich, and into coffee dates. I had a real problem dealing with that. And I realized that I had to deal with my own confidence issues to be able to get my child to mix with her peers, and I would have to take her to birthday parties, which terrified me.'

When I met a number of people heading preschool, their concerns were the parental expectations that they had to deal with. Kiran Tara flagged the obsession with TV viewing. 'They say my child is very busy with the TV and is learning so much from it. "I put on a lot of children's programs and *Chotta Bheem* is teaching them so much, so could you also introduce those in school?" Then there are others who say, "Madam, Smart Board toh bahut zaroori hai, uspey sikhaye inko. My child is a genius! The minute my child sits down in the car I give him the phone and he knows exactly what to turn on and work with, so he can draw and he can play games on it." And this is your two to three-year-old. Parents complain, "My child does not want to play outdoors. It's too hot outdoors! So why do you take the child out when they can play games inside".'

Sonya Philips believes that parenting pressures have changed. 'It's the rat race for school admissions. Their whole focus is—will my child get into the big school, and that's their worry and I can totally understand that—because it is a worry—and big schools are now taking younger and younger children because they are forming their own early years' programme which are most inappropriate to the best of my knowledge.'

'They think that pushing the curriculum down is what needs to be done. That is not how children learn, and it comes with a heavy cost to their well-being. I have no trouble convincing any parent who comes to us why we don't do "academics" in the early years. They trust me and respect that decision. But come age three and above and they are in that trap. What to do—the big school wants them to know their alphabet, the big school wants them to write their name, and know their numbers. So it's a helpless situation.'

Parental pressures also extend to moments of celebration. Ask any parent of young children about the pressures they face while hosting a birthday party for their one-year-old and you can see their eyes glaze over. Unsurprisingly, they feel intense amounts of pressure to keep up with their peers. There was a time when having your child's friends and parents over to your home, organizing a treasure hunt, a game of football, party games, homemade birthday cakes, and fun kiddie food would be deemed a great party! Not any more.

Sabina tells me: 'The birthday party industry is one to be reckoned with. You might host a party at a play centre, where the entry fees is paid by you for all your guests. Technically, it's a play area but once you step inside, it is a cluster of experiences. Let's say you invite up to fifty kids, fifty mothers would come, and they would bring fifty maids. So you'd cater for 150 people. There are separate food boxes for the maids, for the mothers there is catering from Kwality, there's Thai, Chinese, and there's kiddie food, popcorn, French fries, Maggi, and margherita pizzas. Happy junk food. Then you have attendants in the play areas taking care of the children and the maids, and for mothers there are pedicure stations in case they fancy putting their feet up.'

I was aghast to learn that return gifts can cost up to ₹5,000 and the possibilities range from inflatable swimming pools, leather bags with a rainbow, and *Hello Kitty* merchandise with the child's name embossed with gold sequins—and these are gifts for two-year-olds. And then, of course, there are parties hosted at farmhouses which have swimming pools, jugglers, fire eaters, and a giant wheel. Sabina shrugs, 'You spend a fortune. We haven't celebrated her birthday so far. We just don't know how we will manage it.'

How do preschools attempt to deal with the way birthday parties are celebrated by their young students? Can they curb this party opulence? Kiran has tried, 'We have a policy and have tried to educate the parents in restraint in such matters, but parents come and say, "Hamara ek hi bacha hai, koi friends nahin hain"—we have one child, who has no friends—so please let him celebrate at school. Eventually schools have to give in because parents get very upset, and the promoters don't want them to take the child out.'

'It is so sad. The child doesn't even know what is happening. It's just…put on a funny hat and celebrate your birthday. I think if we look back to the birthday parties we attended, it was just so much fun. Apart from balloons I don't remember anything else at birthday parties; homemade cakes, everything was homemade, treasure hunts, balloon fun, and outdoor fun. It was never too hot or too cold for us. We were running around, we fell, we got up. Children are not allowed to fall today. If the child falls down the parent will come and scream at you. "What were you doing?" When it happens in school, the school is held responsible.'

Sonya has started a lovely practice at her school. 'We have the child make a playdough cake, she gets to do it since it's her birthday and then we request the parent to give a book for the class—the child brings a gift instead of feeling I have to get a gift. It's about giving. Mothers say, "We'll send the book but don't ask us to read". And the kind of books they send! It's a new phenomenon. This wasn't the case even up to three years ago, they knew the kind of books to choose, they knew how to come and read to the class, but now no more.'

The pandemic has not doused the fires of the birthday party industry and the internet is alive with companies offering ideas for virtual parties during lockdowns. They range from themes around popular movies like *Frozen* or the ever popular *Peppa Pig*, to adult parties where friends are invited to send videos, drink alongside, and play games such as charades, scavenger hunt, and the more sophisticated virtual escape rooms. One has to admire their entrepreneurship.

COMPETITIVE PARENTING

The competition we feel in our lives has shaped our behaviour as parents as well. As parents, we are increasingly concerned about how our children 'do' as opposed to 'who they are'. A word of caution comes from Madeline Levine, author of *The Price of Privilege*—always be aware of the dangers of competitive parenting. This exhibits itself when 'parents obsessively compare notes on developmental milestones, social progress, and academic achievement'[5].

I suppose that happens when you regard your child to be an extension of yourself, much like a prized possession. Their success becomes your success. Their triumph becomes your badge of honour and their achievements are not their own but yours. This is a tough one to get around. In a sense it's always been there, but not in such a heightened way as we see and feel it today.

My first experience of this was when my son was a baby. My colleague at work had a baby girl, in fact his wife and I were in hospital together so our children are born just days apart. Every four weeks or so he wanted to compare notes: was my son sleeping through the night because his daughter was. Could he grip my finger? Did he understand it was time to change his nappy? Was he able to hold his head up by himself? Was he rolling over? Was he crawling? Was he eating solid food? Needless to say, I found my head spinning as his young baby daughter was streets ahead of my son. My levels of anxiety were out of control when it came to potty-training. I took to avoiding my co-worker and finally shared my misgivings with my husband about possible developmental delays. His response was, 'If he is still wearing nappies at eighteen, we'll worry.' Back then I didn't take kindly to this flippant remark, but years later, when one by one all my fears were laid to rest, I could see, annoyingly, that yet again, he had been right.

Samina has experienced this competition first-hand, particularly amongst mothers. 'It tends to be about how much their child can do, and demands are made on the preschool to fill gaps they perceive. They don't think twice about interfering. When children start nursery for

---

[5]Madeline Levine, T*he Price of Privilege: How Parental Pressure and Material Advantage Are Creating a Generation of Disconnected and Unhappy Kids*, New York: Harper Collins, 2008.

Parenting in the Age of Anxiety

five days, there are some children who were slightly older and there is a huge complaint that "our" children are being bullied. That's so natural, that's the real world scenario. They will meet older children on a slide and they're going to have to deal with it. Clearly, they don't go to parks, they go to play areas or birthday parties.

'As parents we have focused on speaking to our daughter in Hindi primarily, with some English thrown in. But I keep getting asked whether I am teaching her enough English. I'm not worried about that, gradually her vocabulary, which is very rich, will get richer. But you're constantly made to feel as if you're not doing enough.'

As a head of a preschool, Kiran is emphatic—'Parents are very competitive. I think it's about keeping up with the Jones'. It's always happening, "Usne wo wala dress pehna tha, who kahan se tha, kitne ka tha. Wo uss car mein aatey hain, kya make hai uss car ka? Hamari car usse badi hai"—she was wearing that; where was it from; and how much was that for? They came in that car, what are its specifications? But our car is bigger.

'Normally we would tell our children to pick up their own bag. But the mother would tell the child, "Aap betho apne BMW mein, hum chaprasi ko bhejhenge aapka bag lene"—you sit in the car, we'll send the peon to get your bags. So what's the message we are sending? What are the children going to grow up to be? And will they parent in the same way?'

Hand in hand with the competition goes the intervention by parents who are constantly hovering over their children and interfering with the preschool, on the soccer field, and in the activity classes they have set up.

Research reported in the journal *Developmental Psychology* concluded that it's best to let children fight their own battles. Parents who 'hovered' over their toddlers in an excessively protective manner produced less likeable, more incapable, and academically underperforming children.

There is an achievement culture, and it is escalating, no doubt. We want them, even at this young age, to excel and achieve at a number of different activities.

ANXIOUS PARENTING

Ultimately, the culture of achievement and expectation leads to anxious parenting and anxious children. Currently, we are nearing peak levels of anxiety in our children at an increasingly younger age. That shouldn't come as a surprise when you see the levels of anxiety amongst young parents. The anxiety ranges over myriad questions. What did my child do at preschool today? Did she eat? Should she be checked for celiac disease? Is she glucose intolerant? Lactose intolerant? Is she learning enough? Young children between the ages of two and four are being packed off to communication workshops, swimming, and golf, yes golf, at four.

Kiran despairs about the anxiety around food and safety. '"My child should not fall down, she should not cry at school." So we're putting them into a little glass cage. They don't build resilience. Also when you look at the maid culture, today every classroom in a preschool will have teachers and a maid attached to it, and the maid will be doing so much. When I ran my preschool, my teachers did everything, indoors and outdoors. Language built up quicker and strong bonds were forged, and today that is missing. Today, a child cries, you hand the child over to a maid, "issko chup karado"—make her stop crying.'

'Parents don't know which way to go. Preschools are in a race and they don't guide the parents because they want the numbers. Numbers and alphabets are starting ridiculously early. We have rigid little classrooms with very little play material. But if you look at a Reggio classroom (a non-traditional classroom with no assigned seats), it's magical. Can we not bring back the magic of childhood, where we let children make choices, instead of pushing them according to the timetable, and that's making both the parents and children anxious.'

Anxious parenting is complemented by parenting being shouldered by nannies. Sonya feels that nannies have become a status symbol.

'The nanny is there in uniform, she comes with the child and the mother can't make the child wear the shoes, the nanny has to do that. It comes with affluence.'

As parents, Raghu and Fiona took the early decision of bringing up their daughter without the help of a nanny. It was hard going but they feel they have done the right thing. 'We can tell which parent spends more time with their child because they don't have maids hovering around their children 24/7. And the way they talk to their children is different. They don't seem to know their child very well, they're extra polite with their children, almost formal in a sense. Children appear to be more attached to the maid. When the Didi is on leave, the child stops eating, cries for the maid, and the whole house turns upside down. They can't seem to be able to do things by themselves. We are quite happy doing things by ourselves though it takes its toll. We do not have a maid dedicated for her.'

'Also you're getting a different class of maids today,' says Kiran. 'English speaking maids, well turned out, trained by placement agencies in Darjeeling and Kolkata. They help kids do their homework, read stories; they follow the routine that madam has put down, and the food that madam wants the child to eat, and very often the maid comes to the parent-teacher meetings at school. Parents seem unable to manage their children any more. I miss seeing parents do things with their children. You go to a park, you will see mainly maids, and the maids are interacting with each other and the children are playing on their own.'

CONSUMER CULTURE AND SAYING NO

Some years ago, youth were the prime target of advertisers. Today we have a scenario where very young children are exposed to advertisements, and the seductive appeal to buy the products that promise so much. Children as young as four are aware of brands and the power they wield. So a preschooler wants to only wear Gini & Jony and colour coordinate it with *Peppa Pig* or *My Little Pony* accessories. Privileged children get more things they don't need now than ever before.

Anxious parents, eager to make their children happy, feel that children have to be given stuff without making them wait. There is always the aspiration for the next best thing and this can only end in a perpetual state of dissatisfaction.

Toys have been taken over by gadgets in the lives of young children. How do we choose the right toys? According to a study in the journal *Pediatrics*, 'Experts are of the opinion that the best toys for a child are those that foster play between the caregiver and the child. It has warned parents against using digital gadgets as a replacement to traditional toys and games.'[6]

The study also cautions parents on limiting video game time and screen time for young children. 'Total screen time, including TV and computer use, should be less than one hour per day for children aged two and above and avoided completely before they are two. Children under five should only play games that are developmentally appropriate and always be accompanied by a parent.'[7]

The Indian Academy of Pediatrics does not have a stated policy, but Dr Samir Dalwai, former chairperson of the IAP's Neurodevelopmental Chapter, advocates 'Simpler toys for children since digital gadgets not only deprive the child of physical activity but also fail to challenge them. Playing a video game is easier for a child than playing with other children.'[8]

So true. I can remember my son and many toddlers I have known be really happy with an array of wooden boxes, wooden spoons, and different saucepans and make their own imaginative play with them for hours. In fact, at Christmas, he would be more curious about the boxes the presents came in than the present itself.

So, how do we say no? Say it and mean it. It still won't stop

---

[6]Aleeya Heeley and Alan Mendelsohn, 'Selecting Appropriate Toys for Young Children in the Digital Era', *Pediatrics,* January 2019.
[7]Afshan Yasmeen, 'Choosing the Right Toys', *The Hindu,* 16 December 2018.
[8]Ibid.

your two-year-old from throwing a hissy fit if she doesn't get what she wants, there and then. The terrible twos, as that age is called, is when children are prone to having their way and one of the earliest nightmares of any parent is when the crying begins in public, along with the screaming and throwing themselves on the ground, and you feel the disapproval in the eyes of other parents.

Samina shares: 'One parenting rule my mother taught me was—whenever she asks for something, say no. And that's something my mother did for me. So much so that by the time I was eight, I stopped asking for things. So things like nahi mil sakta, baad mein de denge—you can't get it immediately, we'll give it to you later—distract the child, and children forget, like she does. The first time never give it, you may give it to her later if she doesn't get distracted, but not the first time, except food of course.'

Raghu and Fiona have learnt to say no, too. 'If she wants something she'll come to me, and if I say no she'll go to Fiona and say the same thing. We do say no, and she hates that word. She has started using that word against us—she says no to everything we ask of her. Amna have your dinner—no. Amna bedtime?—no. Fiona's level of scolding is much higher than mine and sometimes when she is scolding her I want to run out of the room.'

Bhanu is clear that no means no. 'Before I take him out, I make it clear that today there is no shopping, only one thing, choose what you want, but only one thing. Luckily, at the moment, his obsession is tiny cars and fire trucks. He can't get away with stuff with me. People who spoil him are his father and grandmother. I'm the only one who fixes him and he is only scared of me.'

Sonya laments that since 'Parenting skills are zero, we need parenting classes and parent education. There's a way to be a good parent, or teacher, or doctor. Parenting is such an important role and function. With our materialistic urban life they think that by throwing material goods at kids they are doing well. "Chup ho jao!"—quiet down please—you will get a treat, rather than teaching values.'

And here comes the area of the dreaded D word—Discipline.

Is it getting harder to control our children? Have we given them too much entitlement? Do parents feel they're losing control? Is shouting the new smacking? What is the impact on children? And are there alternatives?

Having been there myself, I know I never felt very good after a shouting match while my son appeared to listen but with the shutters down. I realized explaining why I shouted when I had calmed down, helped me, and I hope it did the same for him. Should we be beating ourselves up over it? We are only human after all and it's a part of the fabric of family life. I believe a little shouting is alright, it prepares children to understand that in the real world people do get angry. Having said that, it's a different ballgame when adults shout at each other. The latter creates a great deal of stress and anxiety and can affect a young child's brain.

We are also creating pathways of learned behaviour which they will emulate as they grow older. Chronic stress levels and the fear that is generated from such discord raises cortisol (the body's main stress hormone) levels, affecting children's brains. According to research conducted by psychiatrists at Harvard University, the development of a young brain is impaired and can lead to post-traumatic stress disorder, among other social problems, if constantly exposed to verbal abuse. According to the findings, prolonged verbal abuse impacts the left brain—the hippocampus. The study suggests that verbal beatings can have as much negative impact on a child as sexual abuse.[9] Having said that, early social experiences lay down neural pathways but the brain keeps on developing and positive pathways are possible.

So how do we get our message across to our toddler who is throwing a tantrum or the naughty nine-year-old that is crossing boundaries? Some tips from parenting experts. Be clear and firm. Look at them in the eye, at their level, a touch on their shoulder. Parental authority is important so don't plead or grovel. It's also good

---

[9]William J. Cromie, 'Verbal beatings hurt as much as sexual abuse', *Harvard Gazette*, 26 April 2007.

to thank them when they have followed your instructions.

Samina says, 'I don't use threats. And I don't smack, ever. But I tell her I'm very upset when she behaves like every two-year-old will. And she understands. "Mama bahut gussa hai"—mummy is very angry. I stop talking to her. Then she'll come and pat me and snuggle up and say sorry. She knows when she crosses the line.'

Our children are much smarter than we were. Amna knows at eighteen months what she can and can't get away with. Her parents have noticed that around guests she is as good as gold. No sooner does the front door close behind them, she throws a fit, gets scolded, and if she has gone too far, they raise their level of scolding. 'It's only then she realizes that I have gone too far, I will have to play ball,' says Fiona. We ask her, 'Why you are crying. What do you want? Then she has to explain it to us and that's better than to let her cry. So we tell her don't cry, ask for what you want. It works sometimes and sometimes it doesn't.'

Bhanu believes that a gentle smack doesn't hurt. 'There is a reward based approach as well. There is discipline—Aman has a mind of his own and all hell will break loose if you allow him to do what he wants to do. Tantrums happen and they're still happening. I deal with them. I don't react or respond. If he is crying and screaming and shouting, I let him. I don't cave in at all. I punish him. He knows the meaning of the word and he knows there are different punishments when he has been a bad boy.'

Children are born negotiators and very skilled—adults tend to lose the negotiations every time. I cannot remember my son throwing a tantrum. He was firmly ignored whenever he started throwing tantrums, and pretty soon he realized that this route was not going to work. Parents sometimes take to shouting and then it becomes a contest—who tires first.

So here's the voice of moderation. A little shouting and firmness is not a bad thing. Different children respond to different ways of discipline. It's anger and hostility that is bad for them. Children in shouting, aggressive households grow up seeing the world that way and are primed to interpret everyone as aggressive. Along with discipline, work consciously at putting down codes of good behaviour—being polite, grateful, and always kind to others, and if we as parents follow these codes, the children will follow in our footsteps.

DIGITAL FAMILIES

If there is one thing that upsets me deeply, it's seeing babies and young children being given phones to play with. While working on this chapter I have been observing parents and children in public places more closely. This gesture by parents, of handing young children the phone, is tantamount to getting them addicted. I know this sounds over the top, but here's the thing—a vast amount of research is available that is screaming out at us and I still see mums or maids with prams, in the park, handing the phone to an eleven-month-old, while they have a natter themselves. It's everywhere, especially at busy public spaces—at airports, in hospital waiting rooms, shopping malls, you name it. My husband had to physically hold me back at a recent visit to Apollo Hospital, where a three-year-old was obsessively banging the smartphone in the waiting area, presumably because the battery had died and she was throwing tantrums.

You probably saw that funny old YouTube video of 2011, where a one-year-old is sitting in front of a fashion magazine, gamely touching and swiping the page with her fingers in an effort to get the images to move. At the time the iPad was relatively new and we were still really impressed at how quickly babies who could barely hold a crayon could master a touchscreen. The creator of the video wittingly titled it, 'A Magazine Is an iPad That Does Not Work'. Phones and iPads have become pacifiers, a bit like what TV was to parents in the 1980s.

Research suggests that technology is not the best early experience to fire the neurons. How much screen time should they have in the early years? Is the addictive nature troubling?

An article in *India Today* quotes from a 2018 study conducted by AIIMS and the Department of Biotechnology, Ministry of Science and Technology, according to which, every third child among the 7,000 students surveyed in Delhi's private schools suffers from obesity. 'Cases of mobile phone addiction among children who are beginning to show symptoms of health conditions are on the rise. Many of them are addicted to games such as PUBG. What parents don't understand is that children cannot buy mobile phones on their own. Why should parents give it to them? It is high time this was controlled,' says Dr Saxena of AIIMS.[10]

These are alarming statistics by themselves, and when exemplified by the case studies quoted at length in the piece, there is a genuine fear that this will only escalate. Take the example of four-year-old Rihaan, whose restlessness was difficult to deal with and could only be managed with kiddie videos on his mother's smartphone. There were complaints from the teachers at his playschool that he was becoming increasingly aggressive unless he had a device to play with, and the principal advised the mother to consult a doctor. Rihaan had developed what doctors' call Screen Dependency Disorder, or SDD, a condition that needs medical intervention.[11]

Sadly, Rihaan isn't an exception. Every day, doctors in the national capital get at least four to seven cases of children addicted to electronic screens. Of these cases, children in the age group of four to twelve years of age, more often than not, grow up to be obese, diabetic and/or suffer from sleep disorders, said doctors.[12]

In another case study, the three-year-old child could not fall asleep unless he had played games on his father's mobile phone. Initially, his mother thought he was suffering from insomnia and consulted a paediatrician at AIIMS. He was referred to a child psychologist who asked his parents to keep him away from phones and keep him

---

[10]Priyanka Sharma, 'Kids addicted to electronic screens susceptible to obesity, diabetes', *India Today*, 28 April 2019.
[11]Ibid.
[12]Ibid.

busy with books and toys instead.[13]

According to Dr Aruna Broota, a child psychologist based in Delhi, she sees at least four to seven children every day in the age group of four to twelve years who are addicted to electronic screens. She believes the problem often begins at home. 'Why can't children be allowed to play and run around, even if within the confines of their homes? Rather than attend to them, the parents often take the easier option of handing them a mobile phone or a tablet,' she points out.[14]

According to the *International Journal of Preventive Medicine*, 95 per cent of children in India live in homes with a mobile phone and 73 per cent of Indian children are mobile phone users. Professor Sanjeev Bagai, chairman of Nephron Clinics, explains how children exposed to mobile phones, tablets, television screens tend to turn obese.

'A stationary child playing on a tablet or screen tends to eat more and in 99 per cent cases they munch fried food which has high sugar, trans fats, and salt. These children develop metabolic changes in their body and usually suffer from low calcium and vitamin D directly linked to obesity. Prolonged exposure to screens creates hormonal imbalances in the children's bodies, further impacting their cognitive and endocrine development,' Dr Bagai elaborates.[15]

Studies have proved that children who engage in physical activities show better development of the brain than those who are home-bound and stationary. They stay more focused, develop stronger memories, and are less impulsive.

The parents I spoke to echo this struggle with devices. Sabina admits 'We really don't know how to deal with the issue of the cell phone. She discovered the phone because we were not able to stop the use of our cell phones. We both get messages from our clients about work on WhatsApp...we have a constant habit of looking at our phones, and both of us have not been able to let go, and that's

---

[13]Ibid.
[14]Ibid.
[15]Ibid.

probably how she's picked it up. She knows there's something on the phone that's interesting. So my real problem is to distract her from it, but when she is eating she will insist on watching a story on the phone.'

Sonya holds coffee mornings at her school and shares information on how the brain develops in young children and how the early use of screen time limits their growth. 'It's really frightening to see little infants in a restaurant with this gadget in front so that parents can quietly eat dinner. So the iPad has replaced a babysitter, but at a heavy cost. They have no idea that a passive screen at that age affects their child. Brain studies are telling us that the dendrites develop between 0–5 years of age, a million in a second, provided the stimulation is being given, otherwise they automatically prune themselves. The brain's architecture is being formed at this stage. Language is not learned passively, there is a give and take, a serve and return, as we call it. So, it is like a child asking a question and no one responding to it, and that's what happens on a screen. There is no stimulation.'

There is gratification in all these videos, your brain gets hooked, there are short segments, and it's addictive. This comes at the cost of not having the social skills, not having the ability to use language, not having the vocabulary, empathy, not having the ability to read social cues, and not understanding the feelings of another person. The human brain is being rewired and human beings ten years down the road will be very different from our mothers or grandmothers. We will not be relating to people on human qualities such as empathy, attention, listening, and responding. We won't have those skills, they will be pruned away in our brains. The whole brain architecture is changing at the risk of how society is shaping.'

That's not natural, it's going against nature. It doesn't call for well-being, we will see the negativity in our behaviours, our lack of patience, our quickness to anger, irritation, that's what society is producing. We already see it—where's the tolerance, the understanding, and the compassion?'

But because the early years are the key stage for brain development,

I strongly feel that in those years at least, we should do the right thing in shaping this brain architecture of a child. Unfortunately, the education system is contributing to a downward trend—we are asking a child to sit, to write, to fill out worksheets, to colour between the shapes. Young children have so much more power. Kids are amazingly smart and capable and we are shutting them down instead of allowing for that to flourish. The dysfunction starts right there.' In fact, in most cases, an adult's mental health can be traced back to the experiences from their childhood—good or bad.

'Take a look at the warnings', James Williams, an ex-Google engineer states with finality, 'These products are designed by engineers to grab our attention and take our time, it is unprecedented power.' In his book, *Stand Out of Our Light,* Williams points out how, even as tech companies profit from gaining our attention as users, interestingly, tech moguls don't give their own children access to their products, for as long as they can help it.[16]

This quote from Alice Thomson in *The Times* sums it up—'The philanthropist Melinda Gates told me that her children don't have smartphones and only use a computer in the kitchen. Her husband Bill, the Microsoft co-founder, spends hours in his office reading books while everyone else is refreshing their homepage. The most sought-after private school in Silicon Valley, the Waldorf School of the Peninsula, bans technical devices for the under-elevens and teaches the children of eBay, Apple, Uber, and Google staff to make go-karts, knit, and cook. Facebook's Mark Zuckerberg wants his daughters to read *Dr Seuss* books and play outside rather than use Messenger Kids. Steve Jobs's children had strict limits on how much technology they used at home.'[17] Clearly different rules apply for their own children!

And then, in April 2019, came the warning from the World Health Organization. In a new set of guidelines, the World Health Organization said that infants under the age of one should not be

[16]James William, *Stand Out of Our Light: Freedom and Resistance in the Attention Economy*, Cambridge: Cambridge University Press, 2018.
[17]Alice Thomson, 'Help Kids to Kick Social Media Addiction', *The Times*, 14 March 2018.

exposed to electronic screens and that children between the ages of two and four should not have more than one hour of 'sedentary screen time' each day. Up until the age of four perhaps they could read a book on the iPad with a parent, but not left with the device on their own.[18]

IT'S OKAY TO UNPLUG!

Yes, it is okay to unplug. We are so habituated to what we consider a lifeline of communication that switching off completely produces a sense of fear, and is impacting our relationships with our children.

Dr Jenny Radesky is a developmental behavioural paediatrician and an assistant professor of paediatrics at University of Michigan's medical school. She has researched extensively on the use of mobile technology by parents and young children and how this relates to child self-regulation and parent-child interaction. 'The telephone took decades to reach fifty million global users, and we had *Pokémon Go* do that within, like, two and a half weeks, so we all feel like we've been blown over by a tidal wave of all this new stuff.'[19]

In case you are looking for advice, Radesky and other experts share takeaways from their research that can guide parents who want to improve their relationships, both with their children and with technology. And this is what they have to say, and it's all common sense:

1. Put your phone away whenever possible when you're with your kids.
2. Certainly ban it at mealtimes as well as when you are putting your child to bed. It is disruptive to small interactions with children—a phenomenon that some researchers have dubbed

[18]Emily S. Rueb, 'W.H.O. Says Limited or No Screen Time for Children Under 5', *The New York Times*, 24 April 2019.
[19]Anya Kamenetz, 'Parents, Sometimes You're The Problem When It Comes To Tech Use', *NPR*, 21 July 2019.

'technoference', which could lead to behavioural problems.[20]

3. Stop using the phone as a pacifier, for you or your children.
4. Remember the more children act out, the more stressed parents get. The more stressed parents get, the more we turn to screens as a distraction, for ourselves and for our children. But, the more we turn to screens, for ourselves or for our children, the more children tend to act out.
5. But life makes demands, and sometimes we need to be in two places at once. If you do need to use your phone around your children, then wait for moments when the children are truly engaged and happy doing something else; or if you are in the habit of using a screen to calm your child, instead try a short video or audio track that teaches more mindful calming techniques. Radesky suggests an Elmo 'belly breathing' video from *Sesame Street*.[21]

So once you have put your phones and iPads away, switched off the TV, think about reading. Those who are better at reading in their early lives tended to have a higher IQ score. Language is the core element of communication and therefore children need language-rich environments.

In the film *Arrival* (2016), Amy Adams's character, a linguist, asks the question—'what is the basis of civilization?' The scientist is quick to respond—science. She replies quietly 'no'—its language. Language and words create thought, philosophies, and ways of being, and science follows.

In April 1994, BBC Panorama aired a programme, *The Future is Female*, but on the basis of what? The assertion was that the future is about communication and girls not only acquire language earlier than boys, they are also better at the softer skills of empathy and collaboration. Communication is the formulation of thought—the

[20]Brandon T McDaniel and Jenny Radesky, 'Technoference: Parent Distraction With Technology and Associations With Child Behavior Problems', *Child Development*, May 2017.
[21]Colbie Caillat and Elmo, 'Belly Breather | Sesame Street', PBS Learning Media.

ability to convey and share ideas; expression and the ability to use words effectively.

I hope many of us can still remember when and how we discovered the world of books and the joys of reading. The incredible impact of reading on the development of the brain was certainly not known in the 1950s when my mother took me by the hand and led me into the National Library in Calcutta. I often recount this story and am ever grateful to her for opening this window to me since books, and being read to, were a far cry in the large joint family I grew up in. I loved listening to stories and would wait for bedtime when she would tuck me in, no doubt exhausted after a hard day's work. But Sundays—oh joy! On Sundays, no matter what the family pressures, she would wash her knee length hair and on the pretext of needing to dry it in the sun (time before hairdryers!) we would go to the National Library, where I would be let loose in the children's section and she would find a comfortable place under one of the many old, shady, magical banyan trees, shake her hair loose and read herself.

I can also remember my nanaji's extensive library of encyclopaedias and that he let me run riot through them. I would pore over the colourful photographs and illustrations and ask him endless questions. He read endlessly, even smoothing down old newspapers that the vegetables came wrapped in, reading them while my grandmother sighed wearily.

And the third treasure trove was a small glass-fronted cupboard with some beautifully illustrated books on Greek and Indian mythology, which were the apple of Mr Rehman's eye, our neighbour and the father of my best friend, Zebu Nissa. We didn't have free access to this cupboard, so we would wait for hot summer afternoons when he slept, and then quietly unlock the cupboard and squirrel away a book or two.

Books and reading were my solace, comfort, and joy. Both my husband and I were voracious readers, and have always been surrounded by books. So our son grew up around books, was read to at all times, and bedtimes were special. We always had a book or more at bedtime, very often the same favourite read again and again. I would often fall asleep while reading to him, absolutely exhausted after a long working day.

I see so many young parents focused on developing their children's cognitive abilities in the early years, investing in toys, gadgets, and experiences that guarantee developing their child's brains, raising their IQs, and making them superstars. The answer is really quite simple—read to your children. There was a lovely sign in a bookshop I saw somewhere, which boldly stated: There is no app to replace your lap! Read to your child.

However, with the excitement of carousels of images on a bright screen, young preschoolers are not excited about turning the pages of the book, notes Kiran. 'So I have exasperated parents who say [that their] children don't like books—find something more interesting to give them. The preschool, as a result, has become a great forum for digital things and the more technology we have, the better we are considered to be. Parents are reading less and less. Reading begins when we put our child in our laps, even babies, and read books, and show pictures. It's not happening as much as it used to, and that's where parents needs advice, and that advice has to be hammered home.'

Christine French Cully, in the *Huffington Post*, points to research that shows us that reading helps in the development of brains especially in the child's first five years of life. When kids are read to, their brain cells are literally turned on, and existing links between brain cells are strengthened and new cell links are formed. 'Reading is also one of the best activities to provide the foundational language and literacy skills your child needs to succeed. And let's not forget how reading aloud connects us—reader and listener—in a very intimate way', Cully adds. 'When we read aloud to kids, we send them this message: You are important. This time is for you.'[22]

---

[22]Christine French Cully, '5 Good Reasons to Take Your Kids to the Library Today', *Huffington Post*, 14 April 2014.

Dr Lara Boyd is a neuroscientist and holds the Canada Research Chair in Neurobiology of Motor Learning. In a video explainer available on YouTube, she talks about neuro plasticity, and according to Boyd, our brain is capable of change beyond childhood; even when we are silent there is brain activity. Every time you learn a new fact, or a new skill, you change your brain! When we use our brain while reading, for example, chemical signals between the neurons result in improvement, new networks are created, and changes in the brain structure can be seen.[23]

You might argue that we live in a digital age and physical books are passé. Think again. Research has shown that in an era of automation, only those with the soft skills of communication, interpersonal skills, and leadership will succeed. Reading, immersing oneself in stories, poems, and visuals counteract declining attention spans amongst children. The written word goes into our short-term memory, but visuals are etched into our long term memories—and here's the thing, 90 per cent of the information transmitted to the brain is visual.

Storytelling is so much more important in this digital age because it's evocative, and it's visual. Our brains process visuals about 60,000 times faster than they do text, and good stories are essentially visual and imaginative for our children. The more stories children hear, the more they imagine, think, visualize, and perceive—all the other benefits of reading aside.

So without further ado, head off for the nearest bookshop, encourage your child to browse and buy, find a library (tough one, I know), or better still, start a community library with a group of like-minded enthusiasts. Now we have so many beautifully illustrated and richly contextual children's books not just in Hindi and English, but in all the regional languages. A few generations ago we grew up seeing European children in the pictures and illustrations. Our frames of reference became the antics of English public school children and

---

[23]'Your Plastic Brain, Lara Boyd, Professor, Centre for Brain Health', SVOD, 24 June 2018.

it certainly alienated children from their context. Not any more.

And remember it's good for you as a parent too. The final word comes from a study published in the *Journal of Development & Behavioral Pediatrics* which states that parents 'who regularly read with their children are less likely to engage in harsh parenting and their children are less likely to have attention problems'.[24]

HELPING PARENTS RAISE HAPPY CHILDREN

Educators and early childhood specialists are calling for supporting parents with parenting workshops and, indeed, many schools have taken the initiative to provide a range of such services. What are the kinds of questions that parents are asking the specialists? It ranges from the serious to the ridiculous.

How can I communicate with my child? Is it enough to take him to the park? I am anxious because I work full time and my maid will have to do this for me. Food seems to be a major concern, notes Kiran. 'The complaint always is, "Bhai wo toh khata nahin hai"—my child doesn't eat at all. I have seen over a dozen two-year-olds in my school eating mashed food even at that age. And it's been run through a food processor at times. So how will they develop the habit of chewing? It doesn't help that meals are not shared as a family. For us, one mealtime had to be with the whole family because that was our conversation time. Sadly, now meals are often in front of the TV.'

Sonya has had questions like, 'What should I do if my child is not listening and wants to be on the phone at mealtimes. He will not eat unless the video is on. Put *Peppa Pig* and he will eat, what should I do?' Or, 'Sonya, do you have any suggestions what to do if your child refuses to sit on a small seat on an airplane and they only want a big seat, how do I tell him that the Indigo flight going

---

[24]Manuel E. Jimenez, Alan L. Mendelsohn, Yong Lin, Patricia Shelton, and Nancy Reichman, 'Early Shared Reading Is Associated with Less Harsh Parenting', *Journal of Developmental & Behavioral Pediatrics*, 2019.

to Shimla does not have business class?' It's bizarre questions such as these that are their challenges. Or, 'Sonya we are a joint family and when they are being spoilt by Nana and Nani who are giving them chips, giving them junk food, how do you control that?'

In order to address their concerns, Sonya began to organize coffee mornings. The idea was to share the research on early years—how the brain develops and the role of language in the early years. 'So, how should we speak to our children, how do we listen to our kids? How do we manage behaviour? Instead of saying don't—yeh mat karo—in the negative, how do we reframe it in the positive? For example, instead of "don't run", say "let's walk". Give them the behaviour you want to see, so little tips. Today, you have to teach this to parents, it's not being imbibed from mothers or grandparents.'

She appreciates that many parents' hearts are in the right place, but agrees that they need direction and handholding. 'When I taught in the US there was a whole section devoted to informing parents about conversations around child development and parenting. You can't just blame parents. They want the best for their child, it's the school's role and responsibility to help them,' Sonya adds. 'I think when we hit the wall, the need for parent education will be felt. We are seeing the symptoms of the role of technology and how inappropriate use of it is leading to issues. If it's not controlled and not within boundaries, because technology is good and bad, we may see many other harmful effects—it depends on how it's used."'

Sonal Ahuja runs House of Learning, which offers programmes for parents on a range of topics. So why did she feel the need to do so? 'HoL started four years back and it was triggered by my work with child abuse cases as part of Delhi Legal Services authority,' says Sonal.

'Every day I have parents coming to me and very often it's to do with their child's obsession with a digital device. They come up with the issue after it has become an issue, because they'll feed a baby or a two-year-old by putting a screen in front of the child and then putting food in the child's month. So it's a distraction. The child does not realize what she is eating. My children, when they could sit up, got food and were encouraged to eat independently, spill half, and eat half. I never fed them. Their motor skills start to develop and there is sensorial development.'

Sonal points out that she is seeing many more cases of sensorial deficit these days, in fact, even more than Attention Deficit Hyperactivity Disorder (ADHD). 'Children are not willing to touch sand, feel water, and they develop sensory issues. Now preschools focus on developing these, whereas from birth these senses develop naturally. Children need to touch, feel, and not live in sanitized environments. Parents are fearful of flowers due to pollen and allergies, sweaters have to be the softest, and the child never feels a hard or rough surface...and the senses are being artificially interfered with. I deal with delayed speech, attention deficit, and sensory issues almost every day.'

She makes an interesting point about the transactional nature of parenthood that is emerging. 'My parents were with me, now parents are "for" children. If I'm eating with, I am eating "with" my parents, playing or studying. I was surrounded by a supportive structure. Now parents tell the children we are doing this "for you". You "have to" study because we are paying a high fee "for you". That element of "with" is missing.'

We do live in complex and challenging times and the digitization of our everyday lives perhaps does get in the way of parenting. But at heart, every parent does sincerely want the best for their child. At Sonya's school, Learning Matters, when young preschoolers join, their parents are invited to write their aspirations on ribbons which are then strung up in the play area and left to flutter in the breeze like Tibetan prayer flags. On reading what young parents wrote on each ribbon, I was filled with so much hope:

I would love for her to explore, laugh, tell stories, make friends, be amazed and have that feeling of discovery, and a love for nature.

For my child—here's hoping you are always happy, always free, always independent, and always a good and decent human being.

Our hope is that our children will grow up to love learning plus work well with others.

I pray for him to be happy, smiling, secure, able to apply himself, and continue being curious.

I hope she will be thoughtful and caring.

My wish is for him to find sunshine and love and have the courage to stick to truth.

Raising kids to be happy in today's world isn't impossible, writes Caroline Knorr, the parenting editor at Common Sense Media.

What makes us happy? 'Supportive relationships, a feeling of self-worth, strong character, and other positive influences are what really matter. And while you can't mandate joy, supporting your child—both online and off—creates an environment where happiness is there for the taking. These tips can help you raise a happy kid in the digital age:

> Get gritty. Grit—the combination of perseverance and resilience that helps you bounce back from disappointments—plays an important role in well-being. Instill what's called a 'growth mindset'—the process of trying, failing, and learning from mistakes. When they feel defeated, their inner voice will say, 'You've got this!' They will need to be given that inner confidence that they can overcome problems.

> Nourish their sense of self-worth. Encourage activities and hobbies that give kids a sense of accomplishment.

> Be grateful. At home, create a culture of appreciation by discussing what you're grateful for.

> Go outside. Seriously, that's all you need to do. Nature is scientifically proven to boost well-being. Just put down your phone, close the laptop, turn off the TV, and go for a walk.

> Foster connection. In the digital age the happiest people are the ones who consistently find a balance between screens and the rest of life. And as the grown-ups, we're the ones who need to model healthy habits. So, carve out screen-free times

at home. Unplug everything so you can make eye contact and really listen to family and friends without distractions.[25]

To all the above I would add, as adults we need to be less stressed out in our children's environment. And we need to start with ourselves, for how can we instil happiness in our children's lives when we struggle to achieve it in our personal lives.

Make your child the apple of your eye, which does not mean that we should spoil them, but they should know, always, that your love is unconditional, and that you are always there for them. That comfort and security coupled with positive affirmations go a long way in building a child's self-esteem. Being overcritical, particularly of a child's efforts, makes them timid about throwing themselves with abandon into life. Relationships are at the core of a strong sense of self and sense of optimism.

The words we speak to our children have so much power. Words that encourage effort, words that acknowledge small acts of kindness go a long way in making a child feel good about themselves. There is a strong connection between confident parenting and a happy child. The confidence levels of our children grow stronger as well.

If my grandparents were to read this today, they might wonder at our levels of neurosis. After all, they raised their children without referring to a single book or attending a workshop. Perhaps we have stopped listening to our instincts that tell us how to go about things the right way, perhaps we have stopped spending time with our children. Certain family rituals that we grew up with need to be retained, and if lost, recreated. Create those family traditions—meals together, family vacations, and conversations, being present for each other at important moments, celebrating birthdays, anniversaries, and festivals.

None of us are, or indeed can be, perfect parents. But if the adults at home provide a stable, loving, and conflict-free environment

---

[25]Caroline Knorr, 'How to Raise a Happy Kid in the Digital Age', Common Sense Media, 11 June 2018.

for them to grow in, families can be buffers for our children against the uncertainties of life. We need to spend time listening and understanding whilst setting clear and firm boundaries that nurture their security. And oh yes, never forget, parenting is for life and it's a work in progress!

2

WELCOME TO THE TWEEN YEARS
A LOSS OF INNOCENCE

There was a time when the years between five and twelve were the halcyon days of cheerful learning, family time, and minimal conflict. Children loved going to school, enjoyed their lessons, came home brimming with stories of what they did and as a parent you basked in their happiness and warm energy. But a few years into junior school, and all this appears to shift before your very eyes. Behaviours that we would expect from teenagers are now evident in grades four and five, and in the early years of middle school, when the children are eleven- and twelve-year-olds, we now have a full blown adolescence that parents need to survive.

There is a new term for pre-teens now—'tweens'. It's that time between eight and twelve years when they are not quite teenagers but behave like them. The phenomenon of 'advancing adolescence' is a global one. So if you are the parent of a 'tweenager', chances are that you are suffering a range of emotions that include frustration, despair, anger, and hopelessness. The sweet little child you knew and loved has been replaced by a moody, secretive, monosyllabic recluse who has declared their bedroom to be off-limits to you and all non-tweenaged humanity. I knew my son was still in the house because I could hear music from behind the door that he almost always kept locked. He would shuffle into the dining room only to eat, grunt, and 'aw mum' me, but almost immediately return to the privacy of his secret place.

And it is a secret. Ask what tweens are doing in their room and they will tell you that they are doing their homework or some other activity that sounds constructive. When you point out that the amount of homework produced does not tally with the number of hours they have spent locked away, they tell you they were 'chilling' or 'whatever'—words which can mean anything, everything, and nothing.

I was fortunate enough to speak to a group of parents of this age group who shared their experiences of this early transformation of their young children from primary school to becoming tweens. They spoke with candour and concern about the independence, and the confidence and assertion of the self that their young children were exhibiting.

Bani is overwhelmed by the confidence her eight-year-old displays. 'I was never that assured, and even today I am not as confident as him. That's a bit scary. I was brought up traditionally, and I think everything should happen with time and the mind should be mature enough to grasp things.'

Meena notices the difference in the way they relate to their teachers. 'When my children were four or five, they had their teacher up on a pedestal and she could do no wrong, and it was butterflies and rainbows. As they got older, they started forming opinions—this teacher is not nice, she doesn't like me, and sadly they begin to talk about certain teachers negatively, especially those that they have given up on. I see a huge contrast between the five-year-old and twelve-year-old in the way they talk about school.'

For Priya, the constant questioning was a challenge. 'When they were five, they accepted whatever they were told. Now there's a question mark to everything. Everything we ask of them is countered by a "Why". That shakes me, at times it's good and at times I don't know how to respond.'

Mahi accepts and understands that now they are turning into individuals. 'So now the attitude is—I'm allowed to have my say, it's my right. I also find a competitive streak coming in. I notice that my daughter needs to be good at everything and if the teacher tells her she could have done something better, her response is—the teacher doesn't like me. It has so much of an impact, why?

But many have learnt from their children, too. Naresh's nine-year-old has always had a mind of his own. 'He's always known what he wants and what he doesn't want. I remember we used to go to toy stores when he was much younger and he used to know exactly which toy he wanted, walk in, pick it up, and walk out. No distractions. I would be salivating and he would be focused.' According to Naresh, his son has also developed the ability to be assertive and vocal, and displayed empathy and a clear sense of achievement and purpose. 'Earlier we used to impose our ambitions and aspirations on him and that never worked. We've stepped back, we've learnt from our own parenting, and now he aspires to and achieves what he wants to do.'

Overall, it was the assertion of the ego that disturbed many parents. 'The I, me, mine appears. This is "my room". I still don't say that my bedroom is "mine". He is eight years old and he claims that nobody is allowed to be in his room,' confides Bela. 'He fought to be able to sleep in his room and we were worried he might be afraid of being alone in the dark! That's an adolescent trait. I see it as a loss of innocence.'

So why is it happening earlier? Growing up has accelerated, and we have the phenomenon of Advancing Adolescence or Compression, as it is referred to in the US. In 2009, Mintel, a marketing team coined the term KGOY and KGOYF. [1] The full form is Kids Growing Older Younger and Kids Growing Older Younger, Faster. So what does that mean?

Pooja Jain has had several years' experience as the head of a junior school, and has observed this acceleration. 'What my nieces did at eighteen, my daughter is doing at fifteen. I can see it with every successive class. It's due to the exposure to the world, and unfortunately children are in such a hurry to grow up. Information and resources are so easily available that they are bringing about this change in themselves. And it's manifesting itself physically. Girls are reaching puberty as young as eight, nine, or ten. In schools we have

---

[1] Paul Twite, 'Analysis: Experts divided on KGOY factor', *Campaign*, 4 March 2003.

had to shift our education on what is happening to their bodies much sooner, to younger classes.'

A survey conducted by the Federation of Obstetrics and Gynaecologists Society of India, FOGSI, found that the age at which girls hit puberty in urban India had dropped. It was found that 80 per cent of girls in cities are reaching puberty around age eleven— two years earlier than in the past. Today, one out of three female children experience early maturity. Growing up earlier than scheduled has become a matter of concern for parents and paediatricians. In discussions with parents and teachers it was evident that in many cases girls get their first period as young as eight or nine years of age.[2] This raises many questions on what parents and schools can do to prepare girls for this major change in their lives. More on that in a moment, but first let's look at what puberty is.

Puberty is a phase of life marked by the emanation of sexual hormones characterized by physical and psychological changes. The physical changes are evident in girls as breasts begin to form, and in boys testicles begin to grow, as well as underarm and pubic hair. There are hormonal changes as well, and all of this combines to influence adolescents psychologically and behaviourally.

Dr Anjila Aneja of Fortis La Femme draws attention to the contradictory strands of behaviour constantly striving for independence yet simultaneously demanding special attention and acceptance from parents amongst adolescent girls. She notes how 'bodily satisfaction, looks, and image become a major concern for children at this age, and many suffer from low self-esteem'. Further, according to Dr Aneja, 'Trying to fit in with the peer-group, copying the habits and behavioural patterns of the conventionally accepted and popular seniors and peers, as well as withdrawing into isolation when one realizes fundamental differences or is unable to get the desired results, are some of the common features many adolescent girls go through.'[3]

---

[2]'Girls are reaching puberty earlier than before, and here's why it's an alarming trend', *Hindustan Times*, 6 June 2018.
[3]ANI, 'Why is early puberty a growing trend among Indian girls', *Rediff.com*, 7 July 2018.

As educators we have experienced how puberty appears to manifest itself in a much more pronounced way in girls. They are coming to terms with monthly periods, possible cramps, and discomfort, and this, according to Dr Aneja, 'results in increasing mood swings, a rush of excitement, anger, anxiety, and sometimes depression'.[4]

'Early puberty reflects the maturity of the brain. So, when young girls are exposed to adult information on TV or on the internet, their brains mature faster, which is believed to trigger puberty,' says Mumbai-based gynaecologist Dr Jaydeep Tank. 'The trend is here to stay, so our children should be equipped to handle this phase in a better way. The importance of sex education in today's time can't be emphasized more,' says Dr Tank.[5]

So why is it happening? Many theories abound, which range from lifestyle changes, sedentary childhoods, environment contamination, use of oxytocin in the adulteration of milk, and the use of pesticides. It appears to be a worldwide phenomenon with an array of social and environmental factors causing it.

Mona Chalabi, a data journalist, refers to a study by Dr Marcia Herman-Giddens, which tracked the average onset of puberty starting in the 1860s. Chalabi's writing presents both thorough research and revelations. In the 1860s, according to Herman-Giddens, girls started their periods at 16.6 years of age. By 1920 it had dropped to 14.6 and in 1950 decreased to 13.1 years. The downward trend continued and in 1980 it was 12.5 years and in 2010 had dropped to 10.5 years.[6]

Similar sets of figures have been reported for boys, albeit with a delay of around a year. In 2012, another study, also by the American Academy of Pediatrics, looked at more than 4,000 boys in forty-one US states. Previously, eleven-and-a-half was generally seen as the age boys hit puberty. Like for girls, the explanations put forward were

[4]Ibid.
[5]Harsha Chawla, 'Puberty much earlier', *India Today*, 22 June 2010.
[6]Mona Chalabi, 'Why is puberty starting younger?', *The Guardian*, 4 November 2013.

Parenting in the Age of Anxiety

focused on diet and exercise,' Chalabi writes.[7]

Educators have observed this and Namritha Rathee, the erstwhile head of a junior school in India, confirms it—'Girls are getting their periods earlier and parents in some cases don't explain to the child the biological reasons. They tell her, "It's okay you've got hurt, don't tell anybody it's happened". Kids can understand what is happening to their bodies, there needs to be much more open discussion about these changes across the board.'

Once you have your period earlier than most, your life as a young girl changes in so many ways. Pooja Jain tells me how nine-year-old girls are grappling with what is happening to their bodies, and how, because no one has had a conversation about this with them, it is leading to confusion and frustration.

'They feel different. There's a silence. They believe sometimes that they're being punished and they are the only ones who have got it. Girls talk and they can be brutally upfront sometimes. So they will ask, "You've got it, but I haven't—is there something different about you, or me?" And that's sad. More and more eight- to nine-year-olds are faced with this. You are growing up much faster physically, but mentally you are still a child, that's a tough disconnect for them to deal with and for their parents. You don't know whether to treat them like an adult or like a child, and between the teens and the tweens, all of that's getting blurred.'

I think back to my own experience of having my first period. I was at an aunt's house, playing with my cousins. My mother had not prepared me for what was to come. My aunt and cousins were confused and while they gave me a sanitary napkin, there was no explanation about what had happened to me. I can still remember the fear and anxiety and the myriad thoughts that clouded my mind. Had I done something wrong? Was this a punishment in some way? Was I going to die? Was I really ill? It wasn't till the following day that my mother, a trifle clumsily, tried to explain to me the concept

---

[7]Ibid.

of puberty. But it was only when, a few months later, I was able to discuss it with other friends that the fears abated. I would sneak off into the chapel at school and pray fervently to Mother Mary to make it go away. Convent school does that to you! Needless to say, those prayers went unanswered.

In the early 1990s, as a school leader, I was asked to advise a teacher on a young girl, ten years old, who had showed a dramatic downturn in her academic performance. She had become withdrawn and stayed away from school. When the teacher began to probe gently, the girl broke down and shared her fears and anxiety. She had started her periods, no one had explained to her why or what it was and her mother told her it was 'dirty' and was not to be spoken about. Just like me, she felt she was being punished for something. It was only when the teacher explained puberty to her that she broke down, this time with relief, and in the weeks ahead we saw her reverting to the confident and happy child she was.

Luckily, there are enough resources and initiatives today to introduce children to the subject of puberty. Sharmila, a gynaecologist and mother, used a comic book called *Menstrupedia*, by Aditi Gupta and Tuhin Paul, to introduce the subject of puberty to her daughter. 'It's a comic book which addresses topics which I could not handle. I wanted my daughter to be prepared that whenever it happens, she would understand what is happening to her, she would embrace it, and she would see it as normal. Perhaps using a book is a bit of a cop out, but I felt comfortable in introducing the subject using a book. I told her this is a nice comic, please read it, and then she came to me with questions and it brought us closer together. She knows that I am the go-to person for things she is confused about and that she can talk to me about it, I am accessible and am there for her.'

'Menstrual hygiene is a very important risk factor for reproductive tract infections. But in India, only 12 per cent of girls and women have access to hygienic ways of managing their periods—I was one of them,' says Aditi Gupta, the author of *Menstrupedia*, in a Ted Talk. 'The comic book helped in creating an environment where menstruation ceased to be a taboo. Many of the volunteers took this prototype themselves to educate girls and take menstrual awareness workshops in five different states in India. And one of the volunteers took this prototype to educate young monks and took it to this monastery in Ladakh.'[8]

How and when do we introduce children to the birds and the bees? What is the right age to have 'that talk' with your child about sex? 5 per cent of pre-adolescents get their information about matters sexual from their mothers and 1 per cent from their fathers. Sex is the most natural process in the world but we are so bad at talking about it. Children grow up with insufficient information about their bodies and sometimes grow up with a sense of shame.

Should the conversation be led by the child? Should it follow a developmental agenda? Quite naturally, it starts with questions about gender differences and body changes. Small children are fascinated with their own bodies and those of others. They are into touching themselves and we need to know how to deal with this, to be able to distract them and not punish them. It is so important to not connect shame with children's bodies as it affects how they relate to their body and themselves. Shame, as many of us are aware, is felt even at a young age.

Parents need to prepare their children, and schools have to introduce information and discussion about puberty and the changes the students will experience, before children undergo these changes. Of course, it all depends on how it is done. Vanita, a student, recounts, 'Our first sex education class was in the sixth grade and that was co-ed, we weren't divided according to gender. We were shown a Disney video on menstruation, so it wasn't great. Snow White became Snow Red—it was such a funny video, she's like combing her hair and she's having cramps, it was hysterical! Of course, now all the girls we know get their information from the internet!'

There are schools that are approaching this with sensitivity

---

[8]Aditi Gupta, 'A taboo-free way to talk about periods', TedxGatewayWomen.

and care and getting it right. Rajani Khanduja, a counsellor at St. Mary's, shared that 'Sessions on menstruation and hygiene are done intensively with the girls, and we start with class four'. On why it is done separately for boys and girls, Rajani adds, 'We start with the girls separately first because it's sudden and intense and we don't know how they are going to respond. There is no silence around it. Class nine presented an assembly on demystifying menstruation and the whole pad thing.'

Janani, a teacher and counsellor at the Shri Ram School in Gurgaon, recounts her experience of breaking the silence around periods and extending that understanding to parents. 'It started with two kids running around in school, looking for pads, not being able to find them—and in their frustration they came up with the idea of a "period box". They decided to have a circle time on it, and asked questions—why are there no pads accessible in the classroom? Why do we have to go to the nurse and ask for a pad which is then given to us wrapped in newspaper, or worse, a black plastic bag? One of the kids said, "It's shameful if we have to feel shameful about this, after all the growing-up workshops we have had."'

Janani recounts how the girls first had a circle time to ensure that they were all on the same page with their strategy and then brought in the boys of their class for a discussion. They swiftly organized a period box which had pads, panty liners, medication for cramps etc. There was the inevitable opening of pads, the cracking of jokes as the boys tried to get comfortable with the concept. The boys felt the box should be in the teacher's cupboard but the girls refused. They insisted it should be placed in full sight for all to see. In their words—"We aren't going to hide it. We will open it, we will take the pad, and none of us is going to feel embarrassed about the fact that we're bleeding". Once the first set of pads got over, it was the boys who volunteered to get the next set! How about that as an example of student agency!'

It didn't stop there. The boys wrote a note to the parents and informed them about their participation in the period box project.

There was no dissenting voice from the parents. At a class assembly (incidentally for class eight), the principal addressed the entire staff, and the students told their teachers why they thought this was important to them and the girls told the sports teachers sitting there that—"Sir, the next time I come with my diary, I will not say I am not well, I will just tell you I have my periods. You've got to deal with it if you're uncomfortable, I'm not.'"

In sharp contrast, in another school, when the girls requested for a pad dispenser in the girls' washroom they were dismissed summarily saying, 'What next? A condom dispenser in the boy's washrooms?'

Slowly but surely these developmental changes begin to happen, and are now happening earlier. Neuroscience has shed light on the link between brain functions and adolescent behaviour and it is a relief to see the rationale behind all these changes that we can understand better now.

Madeline Levine, in *The Price of Privilege*, explains how young people at this age are beginning to think both logically and in the abstract, additionally, sex and stress hormones are beginning to kick in and negotiating becomes an important skill.[9]

In adolescent brains, the pre-frontal cortex is the last to develop. This is responsible for complex behaviours including planning, decision making, and controlling emotions and impulses. Needless to say that as we live with our tweens or teach them, all of the above are markedly absent in our morphed tweenager.

Hormones take centre stage, rebellion begins to turbo charge, and they see themselves as the centre of the universe. They are on a collision course with their parents over practically everything. I think back to the flashpoints at home with our son at this age, and the reactions of my husband and my mother who would restrain herself from intervening. My mother used to have a saying, in Punjabi, that when the son's shoe size fits his father's, the father has to accept and acknowledge his son is a man and cannot be hit. She would

---

[9]Levine, *The Price of Privilege*.

say this wearily, as my irate husband sought to punish our son by taking down all his football posters on the walls in his room and stuffing them in bin bags along with whatever clothing was lying on the floor—that magical place where twelve-year-olds put their clothes waiting for the clothes fairy to do the washing and tidying!

Tweens fluctuate between love and disdain for their parents and the desire to be seen in public with their mothers or fathers is very low indeed. God forbid that the parent should show affection and love in public. I once made the cardinal mistake of going to pick my son up from a school trip and rushing to hug him as he stepped off the bus. He disengaged himself as quickly as he could and looked around to see whether he had lost 'cool' points with his peers! I was terribly hurt, and only understood much later that I couldn't take it as rejection, but as a statement of separation which was crucial for his standing amongst his friends. It is hard. You just need to step back and watch them trying to fit in, because approval and acceptance by their peers is the most important part of this phase. They leave you. But they do come back.

Just as children are getting older younger, parents are getting younger, older. This age of compression is about dad and moms being your 'buddies' and best friends. There appears to be a desperate need on the part of the parents to be liked, indeed loved by their pre-adolescent children. It's a nonstarter. It undermines parental authority and makes children feel uncomfortable. Biology, psychology, and the environment conspire to make conflict-free relationships almost impossible. As a parent, you can't do anything right in their eyes at the moment. And if your tween does not say they hate you, you're doing something wrong.

TWEENS TARGETED AS CONSUMERS

As parents a major concern during these years is how to empower our children as consumers and liberate ourselves from the seemingly endless cycle of meaningless consumption. There is a bewitching array of available goods. The meaning of life appears to be to shop. And this is true now more than ever before. And now there is no waiting either. Parents feel that children have to be given stuff even before they ask, and there is no deferred gratification.

In fact, instant gratification is the mantra. There is a prominence of consumer values and the pressure of getting the latest things and constantly aspiring for the next thing. So all of us, adults and children, and families, end up in a perpetual state of dissatisfaction. If children see parents 'buying' constantly, they will do the same.

Namritha Rathee sees how children and parents are much more consumer driven nowadays. 'Take pencil boxes, one finds a huge variety in the classroom, you know these fancy ones where you press a button and a sharpener pops out. So there's a huge competition happening in classrooms. "My partner's got this pencil box, so I also want the same thing", and parents give in. So there again the schools have to step in and say—sorry, we just advocate simple stuff, or we will provide the stationery and keep it for your child.'

The response to messages from advertisers starts at four, if not earlier, and even preschool kids respond to this messaging. These dominate peer group interactions, how they look, what kind of things they have or don't have, all these become really important. What are the effects of consumer messages on children's well-being? As parents, we get trapped into keeping up with our neighbours. This is linked to the belief that 'what' we have is connected with 'whether' our child will be accepted in their peer group—one rests on the other.

Sharmila finds merchandising based on films the toughest challenge with her children. 'Right now unicorns are the in thing. All the girls' clothes and toys, and bags have unicorns on them and my daughter wants everything with a unicorn on it! Brand awareness is coming from peers and from the subliminal messages in the malls. We've had phases of *Frozen*, and every other Disney movie you can think of. For the boys it is sporting stuff—Adidas, Reebok, Nike, and of course, video games, the bane of every parent's existence. They even use brand names for items: I'm not wearing slippers, I'm wearing Crocs. Uncle's Audi is outside…they won't say the car is here.'

So, when life is one long litany of wants and needs, how do parents deal with it? Gurinder has tried the delayed response tactic. 'My girls asked for a Fitbit. We dilly-dallied for six months. Then finally my husband bought it for them. My eldest is very sporty and they really have utilized it fully. They check their 10K steps daily. Now it's the gadgets that reign supreme, and its earphones next, but they are going to have to wait for more than six months for that one.'

Mitali, on the other hand, has attempted openness and frankness. 'The one thing I've started consciously saying is, "Sorry we can't afford it" and there's no shame in that. If they question me about how come, I say that we would need to forgo A and B and C, and maybe your football class will have to go. No more arguments after that.'

Advertisers have been quick to capitalize on this new growing tween market and are targeting younger and younger children with aspirational products that are wholly inappropriate.

In a special episode of HT Brand Studio's series on marketing and branding, Rutu Mody Kamdar, the founder of Jigsaw Brand Consultants, highlighted how brand equity is built early in life: 'The consumer socialization process (the way consumers know about brands) starts at birth. Brand messages are consumed at supermarkets, on television, and other visual mediums. The brain is a reservoir of such messages, which eventually shape our future choices.'[10]

Clearly, advertising to children is a big, lucrative business since children are not discerning spenders. They are a captive audience. In a study that is as relevant today as it was ten years ago, Anup Shah detailed how, in the US alone, companies spend $15–17 billion advertising to children, and over $4 billion is spent by the fast food

---

[10]'KidZania Special Episode—Influencers of tomorrow', HT Brand Studio, 8 July 2019.

industry alone. Children up to eleven years spend around $18 billion a year and tweens heavily influence more than $30 billion in other spending by parents. Incredibly, 80 per cent of all global brands now deploy a tween strategy.[11]

Children have become consumers—is it reflected in India? Absolutely. *Livemint* confirms that new-age parents are increasingly involving kids in household purchases—from breakfast cereals to large-ticket items such as TVs and cars. A recent survey conducted by Facebook revealed that nearly 71 per cent of parents believe that their children have a say in how much they spend on products.[12]

If 71 per cent of the parents are involving children in spending decisions, how should we educate children about the pitfalls of the advertising industry and the media, the subsequent thrust on consumerism, and wilful manipulation of buyers? This obsession with brands and brand consciousness, according to Pooja Jain, comes from the family as much as friends. 'Families and peers encourage this brand consciousness and they also have unlimited access to money and means. This conspicuous display of wealth comes without apologies.... At school, invites to birthdays were getting more grandiose and we had to bring in a policy of only sending simple cards. Conversation in this age group is around money, how they spent their birthdays, where they spent their holidays. No one speaks about travel in India, it's beneath them, and travel for the privileged is always to a foreign destination.'

Children under the age of eight cannot tell the difference between a programme and a commercial, they view the advertising messages as truthful and unbiased and therefore are particularly vulnerable when it comes to junk food and toys. A worrying spin-off of this is the inappropriate marketing to, and the targeting of, young girls. We haven't been deluged by it here as yet, but it's on its way. In the US and UK, advertisers market toxic make-up products made

---

[11]Anup Shah, 'Children as Consumers', *Global Issues*, 21 November 2010.
[12]HT Brand Studio, 'Decoding Children as Consumers', *Livemint*, 8 July 2019.

with parabens, phthalates, and phenols to girls as young as three, exposing them to harmful carcinogenic chemicals and the possibility of early puberty[13]. They are constantly being bombarded with images of what beauty is and form a view of the perfect face, body, and lifestyle at a very early age, which continues into their teenage years and beyond—and none of these ideal standards of beauty are very diverse no matter how much the beauty industry tries. Unchecked, these influences can also lead to low self-esteem and debilitating conditions such as the Body Dysmorphic Disorder, a mental health condition where an individual spends a lot of time worrying about the flaws in their appearance.

Stacy Malkan, author of *Not Just a Pretty Face: The Ugly Side of the Beauty Industry*, asks us to consider the Hannah Montana Backstage Makeover Set for children five to seven years, Barbie Makeup games, and spa services with names like 'Twinkle Toes and Fancy Fingers' that offer manicures and facials to kids aged six and up. In the US, popular hair-straightening products called 'Just for Me!' feature seven-year-old girls on the box, and getting your hair coloured is now practically a rite of passage in middle school.[14]

Pooja Jain is dismayed by the reality shows that depict young children as adults. 'You see these little children acting and behaving like adults. What are we doing? Are we fast forwarding the process of growing up? Are we completely ruining them? Will they ever be able to go back and be children again? They are being objectified as adults. Waxing has started to emerge as a growing trend amongst nine-year-old girls. I allowed my daughter to wax her legs when she was in middle school, which was very late according to her. But now I see that has changed. I see a child in grade four getting her legs waxed, getting her hair done, liner on the eyes, and a touch of lip gloss. And she's not a child any more, not on the outside anyway.'

[13]Susha Cheriyedath, 'Are Chemicals in Cosmetics Linked to Early Puberty in Girls?', *News: Medical and Life Sciences*.

[14]Stacy Malkan, *Not Just a Pretty Face: The Ugly Side of the Beauty Industry*, Gabriola Island: New Society Publishers, October 2007, p. 85.

Combatting focused marketing is well-nigh impossible when money becomes connected with our sense of self-esteem. As working parents, my husband and I had to convince our eight-year-old son that our seventeen-year-old Ambassador car that rattled and banged was just as good as the silver grey Rolls-Royce that had just purred past us. We worked extra hard at coming up with creative and fun ways of having soccer parties on his birthdays, with treasure hunts and games to keep them occupied, since we were vying with farmhouse parties with fire eaters and jugglers! From what I have heard from parents today, the return gifts have made their way to play dates now. So whilst earlier you would just go off and play with a friend, now your parents set up a date, supervise your play, and there is an expensive return gift when the child goes home.

This economic divide creates challenges for many children as those from middle-class families bear the brunt of not being seen as good enough by their peers. Even more alarmingly, it encourages children to look at friendships and relationships through the prism of economics and social biases. I have known instances of students who have been too ashamed to get off the bus to be met by their father on a scooter, or mother in a rickshaw, and have got off at an earlier bus stop and made their way home. There is palpable stigma attached to a low economic status in privileged schools. Students are fearful of this stigma since they might not be able to form friendships because of this. Middle-class parents too feel the pressure of having to compromise on their values when they send their children to elite privileged schools where their children are judged by their economic status.

As parents, what can we do? How can we make children empathetic and kind in an increasingly neoliberal world? How do we help them understand that things that are valuable are not necessarily expensive, and things that are expensive are not necessarily valuable? It has everything to do with our ideas about being successful and what it means to be likeable. Buying things certainly makes us feel happy—it's not called retail therapy for nothing. Buying things is a 'mood repair'. But we have to find the right balance as adults and convey that to our children.

So when your child wants things, incessantly, ask yourself—do they need it? Collectively, parents and schools need to counter this marketing and advertising onslaught. Encourage conversations around brand bullying and media manipulation for a start. Help the tweens to counter adverts and deconstruct them. As parents we need to be with them (difficult as that is) while they watch TV. Pose questions—What do you think the ad is trying to do there? Why do you think this celebrity has agreed to be in this ad? Discuss endorsements—Why is their favourite sportsperson advertising whitening creams for men? Talk to children.

DIGITAL TWEENS

Into this cocktail of the early onset of adolescence, once you add digitalization, social media influencers, and the beginnings of academic pressure and testing, the problems for children in the eight to ten age group becomes even more complex.

When Apple brought out the iPhone in 2006 it changed the face of childhood. A 2021 study conducted by the National Commission for Protection of Child Rights revealed that 59.2 per cent children in India use smartphones, while only 10.1 per cent use it for online learning and education.[15] In a bid to study internet addiction amongst children in India, Rajeev Chandrasekhar, the minister of state for electronics and IT, revealed that 23.8 per cent children use smartphones while in bed, and a significant 37.15 per cent have experienced reduced attentions spans as a result of this.[16]

Internationally, the voices around curtailing access and use of smartphones for young children are growing louder and stronger. In an alarming remark in 2017, Mandy Saligari, an addiction expert in

[15]ANI, '59.2 pc children use smartphones for messaging, only 10.1 pc for online learning, finds NCPCR study', *Times of India*, 25 July 2021.
[16] PTI, '23.8% of children use smartphones while in bed, 37.15% losing concentration: MoS IT', *Economic Times*, 23 March 2022.

the UK, told Rachel Pells how giving a smartphone to your children is akin to giving them a gram of cocaine. Saligari highlights how unfiltered access to sexual content online and social media has normalized adult and even harmful behaviours in children such as sexting, dieting, and self-harm. Time spent messaging friends on Snapchat and Instagram can be just as dangerously addictive for teenagers as drugs and alcohol, and should be treated as such, school leaders and teachers were told at an education conference in London. Even three and four year olds consume an average of six and half hours of internet time per week, according to the broadcasting regulators Ofcom. So what is the solution—the right balance in bringing up children in a digital age? For starters, Saligari and Dr Richard Graham, a consultant psychiatrist at Nightingale Hospital Technology Addiction Lead, suggest digital curfews and greater emphasis on sleep.[17] The internet can be a great resource for kids to read, especially in the absence of public libraries in a country like India. However, as parents, we have to also teach our children about the dangers of internet usage. There are numerous resources to guide you and your children as you explore the internet together, but here are some tips I found useful:

1. Ask your children to follow rules set for the family—digital curfews, no phones in bed—and teach them about malware, phishing, spam, and blocked content.
2. Teach children about the dangers of sharing personal information, passwords, and photographs online; the dangers of talking to strangers on social media; the futility of heated debates on social media platforms; privacy leaks and consent.
3. As parents, you should spend time online with your kids, giving them a chance to learn appropriate social media behaviour. Take them seriously when they report online incidents to you, and keep an eye out for any unusual bills related to internet usage, online shopping, etc.

---

[17]Rachel Pells, 'Giving your child a smartphone is like giving them a gram of cocaine, says top addiction expert', *The Independent*, 7 June 2017.

So what's the right age for your children to use smartphones—this is a question that plagues parents incessantly. Your ten-year-old can make demands and point out that everyone in their class has a smartphone. And wouldn't it be better to give them one? That way the parent can always stay in touch.

We were lucky. I got a smartphone from work in 2001, and since my son didn't want to be tracked, he could not be persuaded to have even a basic Nokia. So as parents, we never actually faced that dilemma that I see unravelling amongst parents today. Babies and very young children discover the joys of smartphones very early now. And by the time they are eight years old or even younger, the hankering begins.

'Many parents seek advice on the right age to give their child a cell phone,' says Dr Dayal Mirchandani, a behavioural medicine expert and psychiatrist. 'However, it's not really about the age of the child, but how mature they are to handle the freedom of owning a cell phone responsibly.'

He points out that ownership of a cell carries the risk of it being potentially addictive. It could also result in the child becoming distracted from studies and sports, withdrawing from social interactions and maintaining a sense of secrecy. It makes our tweens vulnerable to the risk of being stalked, exposed to inappropriate sexual activities, cyberbullying, and unsafe behaviour on social media. And then there is the danger of the unhealthy radiation that phones emit. 'The blue light of the screen is known to disturb the circadian cycle of the body, leading to sleep disorders, impaired memory, and early development of cataract. The constant exposure to stimuli and sensory overload causes a hyper-aroused nervous system or what is known in the medical field as Electronic Screen Syndrome,' adds Dr Mirchandani.[18]

---

[18]Ankita A Talwar, 'What's the right age for a cellphone?', *Indian Express*, 19 July 2018.

There is no one answer on whether you should give children a phone—in some cases, especially with the number of post-school extra-curricular activities today, it is essential. If you are certain that your children will not be distracted by a phone, and you are willing to take them through the experience of owning a phone and the responsibility that comes with it, it might not be as harmful as we think it is. What should be avoided, however, is giving children a phone as a distraction or as a present, especially since cycling, sports, books, and many other things are far less destructive means to an end in both of these cases.

There should be a genuine need for a phone—such as safety. You might be concerned about your child traveling for coaching or activity classes, and in that case, 'it's advisable to give the child a basic phone, where there is none or limited internet access, so that the functionality of the phone is achieved sans the nuisance value of it', says Dr Rachna K. Singh, a clinical psychologist based in Gurgaon.[19]

The real challenge is dealing with peer pressure when it comes to owning a smartphone. If you take the draconian path and totally deny them access to a device, the chances are that they will feel the odd one out in their circle of friends, and the fear of not being accepted can be a terrible blow to their self-esteem. Dr Singh advises parents who are handing over a smartphone to ensure some practical restraints are built in, such as—'Avoid an unlimited data pack, opt for a prepaid card; let your kid shoulder the payment of these extravagances; install software to protect your child's identity; make rules about usage at night time and during family time.' She urges families to have a no-phone policy when going out together and that phones are put aside during mealtimes.

Finally, explain to children the harmful effects of cell phone radiation. Till as recently as February 2018, the International Agency for Research on Cancer, part of World Health Organization, classified

---

[19]Ibid.

radio frequency fields as 'possibly carcinogenic to humans'.[20]

The facts thrown up by researchers are very distressing, and clearly parents wrestle with how to resolve this. In my conversations with parents of this age group, I found many have attempted to find ways and means of restraining phone usage. Malini's twelve-year-old was begging for a phone with WhatsApp so that he could connect with his friends, fair enough. So Malini tried the middle path—'I've given him a phone where the internet is disabled, there are no social media apps, and he has WhatsApp, which is active for thirty minutes a day. He can call at any time but he can text for half an hour a day. There are two games loaded which he can play for half an hour a day. Parental controls are a great thing. I've told him this is a family phone, your brothers know the password, I know the password, and I have the full right to check everything.'

Surprisingly, it has worked very well. 'I now know which of his friends have potty mouths and I've seen some stuff which I would have been glad not to see, but on the whole he has taken to it much better than I thought he would. In some ways it's actually improved our relationship. He has realized that some of his friends are putting out some unkind edgy stuff, and he wonders about it, which is good because it has come from him. He has friends who have unrestricted access to Tik Tok and Instagram and it's terrible and scary. There are many girls I know who have had Instagram accounts since class five, and they're posing in selfies. It's really sad.'

Gagan follows a path of clear communication and firm consequences with her daughters. 'I gave my girls phones at the age of nine and seven and we've managed it very well. Both my girls do Kathak and violin and they play golf, and are doing well, so I reckon they deserve that treat. They ask, "Mama, can we have ten minutes? Okay, you can have ten minutes, sitting in our room". After a time they get bored with it, and they hand it over. It's kept in the dresser in our bedroom, so we know if any misuse is happening. I

[20]Ibid.

have told them I am giving you the freedom, if you misuse it, I'm going to take it away for good.'

But children find a way. Even if they don't own a personal phone, they have access to their parents' device. Pooja Jain agonizes over thoughtless parents who hand their smartphones to their children in kindergarten and class one. 'It starts from them simply playing games, even five-year-olds, when asked what they enjoyed doing most, they chorused—playing on Mama's phone! Having initiated this, parents don't know how to curb the monster they have created. It begins with this early exposure and spirals out of control.'

I don't think humanity has ever photographed itself as much at any point in our history, the pictures are captured with the specific purpose of sharing them on various platforms. 'Their pictures don't make memories. The peer pressure all the time is to be "cool", to belong, and to do what others are doing. Nobody dares to be different any more,' muses Pooja

It's not all doom and gloom. Namritha Rathee has seen how students can actually use phones creatively while they record events for friends or family or even document events in school as school reporters. She believes that schools need a very well-defined policy on how they want to use technology.

'Children as young as five, as reporters, have documented a school event and they have shared it with the community, or they have documented their journey with a project. And they do it well. They are children, they will go whichever way we guide and nudge them. Children in the third grade are using Scratch Junior, making games, and coding. We use read aloud apps because it helps with their pronunciation, particularly in homes where they are first generation learners, so that they hear what the word sounds like.'

Technology, and particularly the internet, has changed our lives, both for parents and for children. On the one hand there is the incredible opportunity to learn anything! Now, we have an amazing capacity to communicate, to meet new people, and access information that is no longer the preserve of a privileged few. However, it's the unsupervised access to the internet and social media platforms on their phones which is truly worrying. But who teaches and guides our tweens on how to navigate the internet and enjoy the richness of learning as opposed to being drawn into the 'dark side'?

Tweenagers are aware of the pressures of social media. The vulnerability and pressure of being 'judged' by one's peers starts young and that anxiety builds steadily. Acceptance by their peer group is critical at this stage in their development and the requisite number of likes are imperative for a child to feel good about themselves. Girls appear to be more susceptible and troubled by the low self-esteem that is a consequence of a lack of acceptance.

The challenge is—how do you restrict usage for your tween? What boundaries can we put around usage? We ask that question at every stage! For parents, they need to follow the golden rules themselves. About twenty years ago, technology expert Linda Stone coined the term Continuous Partial Attention—a phenomenon that has only heightened in the last twenty years. While we continue to unpack the effects of smartphones and screens on children, the opportunity costs incurred are incredibly high as they choose to stay indoors glued to their screen; premature ageing and damaging impact on self-worth is another effect; and dwindling attention spans are more common now. Rarely do we talk about the impact of screens on parent–child relationships. Stone argues that, as parents continue to be glued to their phones, they are not only adversely affecting themselves but also their children. 'This is the worst possible model of parenting—we are always present physically, thereby blocking kids' autonomy, yet only fitfully present emotionally,' writes Erika Krsitakis. 'When parents lack playpens, real or proverbial, mayhem is rarely far behind.'[21]

So what is the solution to this mayhem? No phones while the family is together, nor at mealtimes. Don't keep phones in bedrooms, charge them elsewhere. When you are with children,

---

[21]Erika Kristakis, 'The Dangers of Distracted Parenting', *Atlantic*, August 2018.

put those screens away. And most importantly—talk to your child about the phone and its usage and why it needs to be restricted. We now know the effects—weak eyesight, carpel tunnel syndrome. Kids see us as having double standards when it comes to using our phones. They see that while adults take a stand on this with them, they are obsessed themselves while preaching to their tweens.

The pandemic, however, changed everything. As learning, living, and working went online, preschoolers, tweens, teenagers, and parents were on screens for their classes and their work, and relaxing on their devices thereafter. For two years children have had to stay at home and spend more time on their phones during the lockdown than they did before. That has left many parents worried about what the 'new normal' will mean for future generations.

Jenny Radesky, an assistant professor of Paediatrics at the University of Michigan, says parents today need to reframe their thinking about screens. Media use, she said, 'has an opportunity to be remarkably different and really meaningful for families.'[22]

'It's amazing watching my own first-grader communicate with his whole class every morning at 9.30 a.m. over Zoom,' she says. 'It's a really meaningful way of using technology in the current context when children feel this loss of their school community.' Jenny Radesky's thread on screen time, made with suggestions from the American Academy of Pediatrics, is just as relevant today as it was during the pandemic:

1. As families reorganize their days to adjust to the COVID-19 situation, we urge parents to preserve offline experiences, which helps families connect emotionally, process difficult experiences, and heal.
2. Make a plan. Talk with your kids about what your daily structure will be, how you will handle stress, and when you

---

[22]Amy Joyce, 'Our screen-time rules don't work in this new world. And maybe that's okay.', *Washington Post*, 25 March 2020.

will take breaks from tele-work or school work to relax and connect with each other.

3. Communicate with teachers about what educational online and offline activities your children should be doing.

4. Use social media for good. Check in with your neighbours, friends, and loved ones.

5. Be selective about viewing positive content, and use trusted sources to find it.

6. Use media together. This makes it easier to monitor what your older children are seeing online, follow what your children are learning, and relax together while you appreciate the storytelling and meaning that movies can bring.

7. Take your child (virtually) to work. Parents might also be asked to telecommute. While expectations may need to be adjusted, this is also a chance to show your kids a part of your world.

8. Find offline activities that help your family calm down and communicate—physical, creative, or playful. Create the space for family members to talk about their worries.

9. Parents—notice your own tech reactions. When you're getting too sucked into news or social media feeds and it's stressing you out, take a break.

10. Limits are still important. The same guidance applies about technology use not displacing sleep, physical activity, reading, reflective downtime, or family connection. Challenge your children to practise 'tech self-control' and turn off tech as adults.[23]

CONTROLLING VIDEO GAMING

The writer Devin Coldeway claims that it's a little-known fact that the phrase 'the children are our future' was actually originally uttered

---

[23]Jenny Radesky (@jennyradesky), Twitter post, 17 March 2020.

by a gaming company executive. Today, gaming is an unavoidable part of a child's life and none can resist the draw. According to Coldeway, around 91 per cent of kids aged two to seven play games. The biggest growth was seen in mobile devices, not surprisingly, but the jump is remarkable. In 2009, only 8 per cent of kids in this range were playing games on the phone. Now, children are gaming every day irrespective of gender and the most popular devices are consoles and smartphones.[24] In India the duration is for at least an hour a day. Furthermore, the biggest growth has been seen in the two to five age range. More kids are playing more games, some before they can speak properly.[25]

Video games are also gendered in their impact. A study by the Norwegian Institute of Science and Technology found that ten-year-old girls playing video games were found to be less sociable than twelve-year-old girls who played less frequently. 'It might not be gaming itself that warrants our attention, but the reasons some children and adolescents spend a lot of their spare time playing the games,' says Beate Wold Hygen, post-doctoral fellow at the institute. Video games are predominantly created by male gamers, and they glamorize violence, sexualized depictions of women, and even misogynistic behaviour—these games add little to children's, especially girls', lives. But as Hygen points out, it is the popularity of video games that warrants closer attention. According to the study, children who struggled socially at ages of eight to ten were more likely to spend more time playing video games at ages ten and twelve.[26]

In the interviews I conducted, students informed me that gaming is largely a male activity, which continues well beyond junior school to university and even beyond. Vanita gave me an insight into how video games affect social behaviour. Whilst at university, she was

[24]PTI, 'Children Spend an Hour on Video Games: Study', *ET Brand Equity*, 16 May 2022.
[25]Devind Coldeway, '91% Of Kids Aged 2-17 Playing Video Games, Says Report', *Techcrunch*, 12 October 2011.
[26]IANS, 'Video games affect girls more than boys: Study', *Business Standard*, 23 April 2019.

sharing a large home with five boys and three girls, and 'the boys did not leave their room, ever, because they were constantly playing with each other. They would go out once a week to Burger King on a Saturday and that was their one weekly outing—they would talk about the games they would play—or dress as game characters! There's a kid's show called *My Little Pony* and that has been sexualized in a game—you dress as a pony—and there are these online groups where you dress up as ponies.'

As a father, Naman finds the violence particularly worrying. 'Violence and PUBG, in fact, the entire PS4 repertoire makes me anxious because some of it is super violent. We have set boundaries that these games are not allowed to be downloaded. There's one game he is permitted to download which he plays with his friends, but the boundaries are set—thirty minutes and he has to earn it. He has to complete some chores and household tasks, so my wife sets certain rules, if you complete these you can have your thirty minutes. The games are those that have been through the scanner and we know are safe.'

BULLYING AND THE NEED FOR ACCEPTANCE

It is around this time that bullying rears its ugly head. In junior school, bullying is largely verbal, perhaps a little physical, and happens for a number of reasons. Primarily, it is a lack of acceptance that results in many children being bullied just for being 'different'. It could simply be the fact that someone is a new student, or is perceived as being 'different' in some ways to the peer group they find themselves in, but it is a major issue for children and educators, and at times can leave the victims feeling the pain of their experiences for a long time. Earlier, the bullying used to be verbal or sadly physical, but now it's virtual and cyber-based, which is so hurtful and everlasting; once it's is there on the internet, it never goes away. Thankfully, cyberbullying is not as pervasive at this stage though sporadic examples do crop up from time to time.

Amina was bullied when she changed schools. 'I was a newcomer. I brought a different energy. I was an outsider. So the other kids did everything to make me feel like one and leave me out.'

What do you do if you're a thin and scrawny kid who gets bullied because he has just come in from overseas with a strong London accent? Jayant recounts 'they used to abuse me using Hindi galis, so I learnt some galis online—and I was accepted! I learnt a few tricks, when I was being physically bullied, I would take my T-shirt off, and I figured they couldn't hit me if I had no clothes on! Another thing, I started moaning, as if my life depended on it, actual real life sexual moaning, they soon left me alone. Boys get bullied about girls, girls get bullied about boys—if you talk to a girl who is "spoken for" you get hammered. You can't talk to every girl, you have to check who she's with.'

Junior school is also the place where mean attitudes, based on clothes and appearance, rear their ugly head. Valli recounts how the class made a newcomer's life miserable because she wasn't fluent in English. 'I used to feel so bad for her, because they would say, "Oh you can't touch her, you'll get infected"—why? It was basically because she did not know English well, and spoke in a funny way. It was easier to be fat than to not know English well. There's a very clear hierarchy, because these were the things that mattered more to those with privileged backgrounds. So okay fine, she's fat but at least she speaks like one of us.'

Malini's first awareness of cyberbullying was when she was eleven years old. 'A girl in our class posted a picture of herself on Facebook. She posted an innocent picture with her laptop. And all the kids were picking on her because they believed she wasn't pretty. Looks played a huge role in sixth grade when social media accounts were coming in, so people who weren't considered conventionally good looking, if they posted a picture, they would be picked on.'

Time and time again we come around to the critical need to have conversations with our children to make them reflect on their actions, on their behaviours, and help them see the unkindness and lack of empathy that resulted in their hurting other children.

We tend to forget the 'silent' pressures pre-teens experience. The transition from childhood to tweens and being on the cusp of full-blown adolescence is a tough one. I was made keenly aware of this when I suggested to some drama students in sixth grade that they develop their own monologues on the pressures they feel, and if good enough we could stage them. The challenge was that it should be under one minute. What followed was a revelation for teachers and parents alike. So here are four voices, all eleven-year-olds, sharing their innermost fears, and above all, seeking acceptance.

Manav

I always feel inadequate. I feel this pressure on me. I think it's coming from my parents, from their expectations of me, but I could be wrong. It could just be me, putting this pressure on myself. You see, both my parents are so, so bright, successful…high achievers. They've been good academically, topping their universities, getting great jobs, and I don't know if I will ever be able to be that. I don't think I will. I feel such a sense of failure. They keep asking me, 'Why aren't you studying? Have you thought anything about your future?' I have difficulty just dealing with the present. The parent-teacher meetings, oh God! Squirming in my seat. Seeing the disappointment in their eyes. (Pause). What if I never succeed?

Mihika

I feel the pressure from my peers. The pressure to be accepted by the so called chic group. They're always having a good time, not studying, breaking the rules, always in wrong uniform, always in trouble with the teachers—but they're considered so cool, they're so popular, they have a fan following like superstar celebrities. I feel a huge pressure to be like them, look like them, and wear branded stuff like them. I cannot handle the pressure of being left out! What if I'm not accepted? I will be so lonely. How can I be as cool?

Anuradha

Have you tried to be beautiful? Have you taken a hard look at that model on the latest cover of *Cosmopolitan*? Beautiful. Thin. Size zero. She looks so happy with life. I want to look like that. I, too, want a beautiful body. A body that can wear the strappy trendy tops and cutaway jeans. I had to beg my parents to get me the latest coloured braces. I hate my hair. I try not to eat. I pass my roti to my dog under the table. And at other times, I end up eating so much! I feel so guilty after that. I'm sure my friends must be making fun of me behind my back. When I look in the mirror, all I see is a fat person staring back at me! Will I ever be thin?

Jahan

I'm the odd one out. They call me the nerd because I like to read. I love books. I can lose myself in the stories and characters. It helps me escape from everyone around me. I top the class. And my peers laugh at me. I'm not quick, or smart, or witty. I don't lead the exciting lives that so many of my classmates seem to. Holidays in exotic places, expensive gizmos, branded clothes. I also know my parents can't afford that. The terrible thing is that sometimes I feel ashamed of who and what I am. Why do I feel so distant? Why can't I be like one of them?

These voices demand attention and want to be understood. It is a difficult number of years for these almost-teens, as well as for parents and teachers, as we attempt to discipline them and assert our parental authority. There is no doubt that we need determination, confidence, and a good sense of humour to get through these years.

Thanks to advances in neuroscience, we understand that they will lack impulse control and self-regulation. In the tween brain, the pre-frontal cortex is the last to mature, and the mismatch between the pre-frontal cortex and the medulla, which controls and regulates emotions, is why teens show increased emotional reactivity. For parents and teachers alike, it is critical to understand this and work on helping their tween get through it.

The change from junior to middle school is a transition from the safety of a close relationship with your teachers and peers to an environment where subjects proliferate, teachers are subject specialists, peers are competing, and they are at the bottom rung of the wilderness that can be senior school. At home they no longer want to relate everything that happened in school.

As teachers, we found the entry to middle school particularly difficult to deal with. They seemed to go off the rails and we found the change incredible in the sixth and seventh grades, with anxiety bouncing off the walls, and little or no impulse control or self-regulation. When questioned, students blamed it on the stress of changed environments. As schools we need to work on how we can help children and parents prepare for this phase—and it is a phase.

Without wanting to pontificate, what we need to keep in mind is that we are teaching character all the time, irrespective of our subjects. Unfortunately, the focus on exam grades begins to kick in and this is the worst time to expect them to work to the best of their capacities. The schools and parents need to focus on teaching these pre-teens how to behave, how to interact with each other, and most importantly, how to show respect. Research and experience have shown us that outdoor experiences, plenty of sport, creative pursuits as well as volunteering helps shape their attitudes and ground them.

As parents we need to understand that when they are little children we give them very little privacy. We over-supervise, over-structure, and control their activities in the belief that we are providing a safe and nurturing environment. But when they become pre-adolescents they begin to create the independence necessary for them to cope as adults. At the same time their bodies are radically altering, hormones are surging, and their brains are restructuring to deal with the transition to adulthood. Therefore, it should come as no surprise when they lock themselves away.

The truth is that tweenagers have a very necessary need for privacy and a need for separation. This need for separation is the first stage in 'letting go' of the toddler who clung to you on the first day of school. Though it may appear they are goofing off, they are in fact spending a large part of their time trying to figure out who they are, and who they want to become. This was little or no consolation for me since I felt shut out and grappled with the pain of rejection.

So, as parents, we have to see our children's need to want to lock themselves away, to keep from us the turmoil within them as they seek to find ways to deal with it, and emerge more independent. And now they have TV and the internet, which gives them control over what they see, and learn, and interact with. Tweens today are constructing their world to deal with the pressures of being adolescents, and they are doing it in the privacy and safety of their bedrooms. They find themselves in an increasingly complex and fast changing world, which they feel that their parents do not have the experience to understand, let alone help them navigate.

I wish I had known this two decades ago. Understanding this need for separation was the hardest bit for me. I didn't handle it well at all, I was impatient and out of my depth. I would have saved myself so much grief had I seen it as a rite of passage. Even through all the hard times, you have to continue to emphasize that you're there for them. And always, always, reflect on your own behaviour.

Their peers will replace parents; they will even challenge us, ignore us, and be embarrassed about having us around. Levine calls this important lesson—understanding that no one is perfect. 'So parents who can tolerate some criticism from their tweens are imparting a valuable lesson: that one does not have to be perfect to be okay. It's important because no one feels less perfect than the young adolescent.'[27]

So think on the mantra—that this too shall pass.
Think on the caterpillar, chrysalis, and the butterfly,
and wait for the adult to emerge!

---

[27]Levine, *The Price of Privilege*, p. 117.

Parenting in the Age of Anxiety

3

THE TEEN YEARS
WHO IS THE REAL ME?

The children now love luxury; they have bad manners, contempt for authority; they show disrespect for elders and love chatter in place of exercise. Children are now tyrants, not the servants of their households. They no longer rise when elders enter the room. They contradict their parents, chatter before company, gobble up dainties at the table, cross their legs, and tyrannize their teachers.

—Socrates

Thousands of years later, Socrates's words still resonate with adults. Despite having little in common, teenagers in ancient Greece sound very similar to the teens today. It's almost as if teen spirit transcends time and resources. Talk to any parent or teacher about the travails of parenting a teenager today and the stories we get are legion. This phase overlaps with the tweens and appears to be the most difficult and perhaps even more challenging than the last for children, parents, and teachers to come through.

A recent episode of the *BBC Radio Women's Hour* podcast painted the scenario really well—there are the moods, the inability to get out of bed in the morning, and the embarrassment of being around parents.[1] We all recognize these moments, suffer them, and wonder

---

[1]'The teenage brain: Seven things parents should know about adolescent behaviour', Women's Hour parenting podcast, BBC Radio 4.

if they will ever end and whether we will survive.

Levine, in her bestselling book *The Price of Privilege*, explains how at this stage, whilst beginning to understand who they are, teens find it really hard to integrate their 'different selves'. 'Unlike the younger teen who often ignores contradictions in the self, the older teen has to struggle to resolve whether she's intelligent or an airhead, introverted or extroverted, a slut or a prude,' Levine writes.[2] They also discover politics, causes, and ideologies. It's a roller coaster with constant mood swings and the topsy-turvy world of romance. As a consequence, the home and school become a theatre of war for many adolescents. Parents and teachers who are in the throes of their teenagers' angst take to meditation, seek counselling, or hit the bottle (I'm joking!).

If we, as parents, knew at this stage why our teenagers behaved in these ways, our desperation would not have been so acute. So here's the thing, neuroscience can now prove that they don't do this because you're hateful and failing as a parent—it's their brain that's working, developing in such a way that it's a default reaction for them to be so. Hmm, I say in hindsight, small comfort. But the *BBC Women's Hour* parenting podcast helped me understand, twenty years after I had suffered blows to my self-esteem as a parent, exactly what neuroscience is telling us. So I thought sharing this gyan might help many others who have been caught or are presently drowning in this rip tide.

Sarah-Jayne Blakemore is a professor of psychology at Cambridge and the author of *Inventing Ourselves: The Secret Life of the Teenage Brain*. Her research clarifies that contrary to what was believed for many decades—the teenage brain undergoes a really substantial amount of development, both in terms of its structure and its function throughout adolescence and it only stabilizes around the mid-twenties.

Her findings bring some much needed comfort: we need to remember that they are changing a lot and those changes are there

---

[2]Levine, *The Price of Privilege*, p. 120.

for adaptive, evolutionary reasons. They need to go through this period in order to become fully independent adults.[3] So a successful relationship will depend on our understanding this as parents, and making the necessary modifications to our responses while waiting for the storm to pass. I cannot imagine that my parents ever sat down to discuss how to deal with my moods or my need to separate from them and focus on my friends with all the intensity of an adolescent. The helplessness felt by parents and teachers at this stage presented itself to me time and time again as parents poured their hearts out in my office and I learnt to keep a big box of tissues handy for these occasions.

The cardinal shift is of course how much they are influenced by their social group. I remember that clearly from my teenage years. Nothing mattered more to me than my precious friends and that was the basis of an ongoing collision course with my father. So even when my son did the same as a teenager, I was completely unable to see it as a phase of development and detachment. I was hurt and pained by his total rejection of what I saw as loving parenting, and his obsessive alignment with his peers.

It is this social influence which is at its highest when they are teens, which quite naturally leads to experiencing and experimenting with alcohol, cigarettes, and drugs. There are also brownie points to score when you nonchalantly shrug and say to your friends that you've tried them all. Long-term health risks associated with this experimentation don't frighten our teens at this stage. For parents this is the trickiest part. How do you address this with your teen when you discover that packet of cigarettes, or they come back inebriated from a party, or worse when you get called to pick them up because they have passed out on someone's sofa?

Another frustrating aspect is to haul your teen out of bed to get to school in the morning and the impossibility of ensuring that

---

[3] Kate Kellaway, 'Sarah-Jayne Blakemore: 'It is, strangely, acceptable to mock and demonise teenagers', *The Guardian*, 25 March 2018.

they get their eight hours of sleep. Frankly, this is nothing short of a miracle. As teachers, we lose our wits attempting to get through to students who are asleep at their desks and no matter how interactive or interesting a class you have devised, you find them yawning at every word you say, shaking the sleep out of their eyes and failing.

But apparently, there is a biological reason for this as well. Teenagers find it hard to get up in the mornings, and unlike young children and adults who bounce out of bed with a smile, our teens find it harder to sleep early and wake up with the birds. Paul Keeley, a honorary associate in sleep and circadian and memory neuroscience at the Open University, writes that in 2004, researchers at the University of Munich proved that teenagers actually have a different sense of time. Their study showed that the 24-hour cycle which determines when you wake and sleep shifts during your teens, reaching its latest point by the age of twenty.[4] Their biological circadian rhythm is changing, and melatonin, which in humans makes us feel sleepy at night, is produced in the brain about two hours later during the teenage years than in childhood and adulthood. No wonder we cannot get them up in the mornings. Now, you would think that a later start for schools might be the solution; it would ensure their much needed sleep. This has also been advocated by the American Academy of Pediatricians who have recommended that schools should start between 8.30 and 9 a.m. Many educators believe this too, and yet our schools start at 7.30 a.m. in some cases—this has been a losing battle with managements.[5]

Along with the impossibly early starts teens also struggle with spending half the night on their phones scrolling—it is a time in their lives when qualities such as planning, decision-making, conviction, and order are in short supply. And there's a reason for this as well! Professor Blakemore explains that 'parts of the brain that are undergoing particularly substantial developments in adolescents

---

[4]Paul Kelley, 'The biological reason why it's so hard for teenagers to wake up early for school', *The Conversation*, 22 January 2018.
[5]Ibid.

Parenting in the Age of Anxiety

are regions involved in decision making and planning, self-awareness and awareness of other people. Those regions of the brain that are involved in these cognitive processes are still developing right through the teenage years and even into the twenties and thirties.' Now that explains a lot about my thirty-six-year-old son![6]

According to Blakemore, 'Adolescents respond better to immediate rewards than to punishment.' Now that strikes a chord. It was impossible to inflict a punishment on my son with the intent of making him feel contrite and remorseful. He would shrug it off, escape to his room, and cut us off, which would pain me even more and I would feel lost. On the other hand, talking to him—not always an easy task—and trying to get him to see the reason for our distress (again, not easy) sometimes did actually work.

And finally, while we know that this is a period of enormous change, transition, and vulnerability, particularly with issues related to mental health, these years are also an opportunity according to Professor Blakemore. 'The changes in the brain make the brain particularly susceptible to change and that renders this period of life an opportunity for things like learning and creativity, intervention, and rehabilitation.'

IN THEIR OWN WORDS: TEEN VOICES

I am so grateful that I was able to gather students for a series of focus group discussions on a whole range of issues that thirteen- to eighteen-year-olds face. They spoke with candour, honesty, and a mature understanding which is often lacking in a classroom scenario. It gives me so much hope that they can confront the environment they are growing up in, the challenges and stresses of this digital world that they are linked to by an umbilical cord, and see it for what it is.

All the teens I spoke to appeared to be overcome and overwhelmed by what they perceived to be various pressure points—from the

---

[6]Kellaway, 'Sarah-Jayne Blakemore', *The Guardian*, 25 March 2018.

ratcheting of academic pressure, to the critical need to be accepted, liked, and to be pretty and popular. They spoke with pragmatism about the levels of anxiety they faced, the panic attacks that followed, the depression and self-harm that they had experienced or seen in their friends. For many, psychiatric help and therapists were a norm and indeed for some it had become a fashion statement. In all of this, the two pillars that have traditionally supported children—parents and schools—appear to be bedevilled by their own problems. There is a sense of a lack of balance. With parents and schools either being absent or hovering 24/7.

Growing up in these complex times brought challenges and pressures and top of everyone's list were parental expectations and the pressure it exerted on their lives.

It's at this point in their school career that the academic pressure to perform really kicks in. All the students I spoke to were unanimous in regarding this as 'insane'—a GenZ term for unbelievable. The impending uncertainty of securing a place at university snowballs into a huge amount of academic pressure to perform. 'Now everything is so competitive, it's all about marks, marks, marks, you have to give so many exams, SAT, NEET, GRE, TOEFL, and at the same time there are school exams, and you always have to be this exceptional student where you have to do amazingly well, as well as have a portfolio for extracurricular and community service,' laments seventeen-year-old Meena.

She is aware that this pressure is coming from her parents. 'I have their words in my head all the time—"Do well, do well, don't get distracted." I just can't seem to concentrate and am so confused about the future. I feel if I don't get top scores, make it to the best colleges, I have let my parents down, and this anxiety just eats away at me.' She doesn't feel proud of anything she has done. 'My parents didn't have this pressure. For us getting 96 per cent is not good enough to get into Delhi University. My parents were toppers, yet in their times they made it to universities with 75 per cent.' So in her last year at school, she is locked in, working on an internship, studying for assignments, midterm exams, and is defeated by the volume of the syllabus, which is just too much to handle.

So how does she feel before an exam? 'I'm anxious, in fact I'm a gone case. I see the question paper and I tell myself—you can do this. But I'm beset by worries. I have learnt to talk to myself, take deep breaths, and try and calm myself down.'

I can remember a knot in my stomach before a paper or before a performance as I waited in the wings to step onto the stage. But what were 'nerves' or butterflies in my stomach seem to have accelerated into a new high with our teens. Deepa, also seventeen years old, is not only anxious about examinations but also about FOMO—slang for the 'Fear of Missing Out'—and had to seek help. 'I do go to a counsellor who is a healer, and that has helped me, for my anxiety has reduced. Sometimes when I am trying to work, to remember as I write, even in school, my hands start shaking. I used to get major panic attacks in seventh and eighth grade, but I haven't had one for a while now, touch wood. It's strange, I also get anxious when people are talking and I wonder—are they talking about me?'

Simran chimes in with the stress she feels—'I do get stressed out and I've stopped playing football as the twelfth grade looms. Real pressure for me is the competition I face. But I try and stay positive and my parents are very supportive. My parents have faith in me and I believe that one always gets a second chance.'

Maina is quite candid and accepting—'Pressure comes from my parents. I come from a middle-class family. We have to achieve academically. I cannot afford a very expensive college so I have to make sure that my grades are good enough to get a scholarship, and that pressure is more important for me than my peers. My peers, who are well to do, are really relaxed about their future.'

Parental expectations can weigh heavy on young shoulders. I can remember quite vividly the responsibility I felt to do well academically since it made my parents and my nana and nani so happy and proud. But it didn't feel like pressure at that time. So responsibility didn't 'translate into pressure because I happened to enjoy my studies, and

I was a good examinee, and therefore good grades came easily. On the other hand, my son articulated his frustration and helplessness when confronted by academic pressure, which was compounded by having high performing parents who had been successful academically. When I shared this with Jehan, who is sixteen, he felt an immediate sense of affinity.

'Yup. I've always had the burden of high-achieving parents. Both my parents are academics. They expect that because of the hard work they put in to get where they are, I should do the same. It's a bit hard for me to get my head around that. My mum is extremely overbearing because of the kind of kid I am—I'm lazy unless it's something I enjoy. I have phases in my passions. My mum won't let me continue soccer, which I love, because it's early morning practice and she says I have to study, but my brother is allowed to go! I argue with my mum about that but her parting last line to me is—"I'm your mother, what I say is the word of God for you!" What can you say to that?'

Not a lot, as it happens, but it is a great punchline and I should have tried it with my son. But sometimes, as in Kala's case, pressure comes with its twin, the G-word, guilt. 'I knew I was not doing well and I felt guilty about that. And there was always an expectation. I was always told at home and school that I was smart, but it never showed in my report cards. But I really really hated the system I was studying in, so I didn't study at all as a result. So I felt guilty, did badly, and that affected the way I saw myself—as a stupid person. And so I behaved like that—a not so smart person! Ergo, my teachers and peers thought I was a bimbo.'

Clearly, parental support on the issue of academic pressure is so important, but what happens when parents don't or can't offer that support to their children? Jasmin recounts: 'The pressure gets to them in a horrible, horrible way. One of my close friends, her mom will constantly scold her for every little thing. Even if she loses five marks! She calls me, crying, saying "I hate my mom, why is she doing this to me, scolding and yelling at me? It seems that marks are the only thing that matter to her and I will only know happiness when I get one more mark than anybody else!"'

And then there are families that actually strike the balance and get it right. Tarini is from a middle-class family and an only child. 'I impose academic pressure on myself,' she confesses wryly. 'My parents want to see me put the effort into my education. I'm grateful for that. So for instance I started out with an E in Higher Mathematics but with consistent effort, no tuitions—mind, my parents don't believe in it, I sought help from my teacher in school instead—I got an A.'

She is aware that many parents don't do that and they value the grades more than the effort. She also notes that in a fiercely competitive environment, academic success results in a backlash from the peer group too. 'I have friends who would get both jealous and angry if I've done well in class. It affects the way they look at themselves. So students really push themselves! Researchers have found that people can concentrate for fifty-two minutes[7] and after that your mind will wander. But many are pushing themselves for up to five hours at a time, that's a miracle! I do an hour at a stretch and take a break.'

She tried doing the 'all-nighters'—going all night without sleep— like her friends and quickly realized that the lack of sleep resulted in her messing up her exams, and she has learnt to value her sleep. The most important thing that helps her work 'is being in a good mental space. If I have a fight with my parents, that wrecks me. My parents started off in a middle-class family and they worked their way up to upper-middle class. I am surrounded by people who come from very privileged backgrounds and I'm privileged too. I've been taught from a very young age to be humble and grateful for what I have.'

I asked the teens that if they could send a message to all parents, what would that message be? Their responses were immediate and, to me, very moving.

---

[7]Derek Thompson, 'A Formula for Perfect Productivity: Work for 52 Minutes, Break for 17', *The Atlantic*, 17 September 2014.

Deepa, who has always struggled academically and had difficulty finding out what she was good at, was very clear about what her message would be—'Even if your child doesn't do that well, look at what they are good at, recognize their capabilities. This kind of pressure could lead their kids to dive into substance abuse, hurting themselves, and anxiety disorders. In India, mental illness is like a stigma, they think it's in your head and they don't see the need for you to seek help. If someone goes to a therapist, their friends make fun of it, and that makes them more anxious. I used to go to the school counsellor in eighth grade, but whenever I went I would first quickly check that no one was watching as I entered her room. Now, I talk about going to therapy quite openly, and I think it's a very good thing that I'm doing for myself.'

THE FUNDAMENTAL NEED FOR ACCEPTANCE

Acceptance is the key to a child's happiness. Acceptance by their parents for who and what they are, acceptance and appreciation by their teachers for their unique capabilities and diverse talents, and finally, and perhaps the most important for teenagers is the acceptance they receive from other students and their wider peer group.

In a privileged school where children from affluent families rub shoulders and share lives with children from middle-class families, there are stark differences in family backgrounds, lifestyles, and values. Children coming from middle-class families with traditional family values struggle to be accepted by their wealthy peers.

For Aman it was the social pressure that got to him. 'I study in a privileged school and one of the challenges we face is assimilating into the economic strata. There are always people who are going to be better off than you and monetarily, they will be able to afford a lot more than you. So there is the constant pressure of "I want that phone, I want that laptop", and you see others having stuff and not yourself, and the extent to which it affects you differs from person to person. From a social perspective you feel the peer pressure and

I felt it more from a materialistic perspective.'

At twenty-two years old, Vanita looks back on her struggles in school where being able to fit in with the crowd was a daily challenge. 'It was a major pressure point for me. There were so many things that I was looking in at from the outside. These kids could go to parties, drink, and wear clothes I couldn't afford. Since the year I started sixth grade, I was not allowed to go to parties or go out at night—which is fine, but everybody around me was doing that already—people were celebrating their thirteenth birthdays in their homes, where they would drink and take photos. I was always sidelined—once you get segregated it continues well into your senior years. I got over it eventually once I accepted that we were not the same kind of people, but it was isolating and jarring in the beginning. They all had lives after school that I was not a part of. It was a huge pressure.'

Vanita's parents were working and money was always in short supply. She remembers the sense of guilt she felt at asking her parents for things her peers had, since the school fees was already very high. It didn't help that her peers were brand obsessed and threw lavish parties. 'For instance, my friend Anita had a champagne fountain for her sixteenth birthday. It was so far from my reality, my friends would come home for my birthday, and we had pizzas and a sleepover! So where's the common ground to talk about?'

How parents deal with their teen's wants at this stage can vary. Some will overcompensate, take an overdraft to ensure that their child does not feel undervalued. Others will take a more direct rational approach and Tarini recounts how her parents put her right on this one!

'When I was in junior school I would come back with stories about, "Oh my friend has all this amazing stuff, a made-to-order desk, stuff in her room, and so many gadgets!" I never asked for stuff, I think the only thing I wanted once was a keyboard for a 1,000 bucks, and they said "No", and I said, "Oh, okay". I never thought people with privilege shouldn't have what they do. My parents taught me tolerance, which I now realize is so important. And so I choose not to go around and throw moral stones at people, I don't feel the need to.'

Parties, branded stuff, and gadgets apart, the real challenge comes with access to technology. Geetha, from Bangalore, thinks back to when she joined school and was the first person without a smartphone. 'It was hard not to have access to that kind of world because that meant people were forming connections after school in the virtual world and I was missing out on a lot of fun as well, and that troubled me. Then when I got a phone—it didn't support WhatsApp, and I was constantly struggling to catch up with the latest technology which was beating me every single time. I never had Facebook on the go, I missed out on Snapchat and I was out of the loop and out of the trends which formed such an integral part of our culture. It hindered my socialization.'

She clarified that she wasn't shunned because she didn't have the latest gadgets, she was just not privy to that lifestyle, and so, does she regret it? 'In hindsight, no—what seemed very important at that time seems very inconsequential now. But during that time it hit my confidence for I felt I did not belong a 100 per cent to my peer group—that was a struggle. You felt the difference. And because my parents couldn't understand this vital need to blend in and be accepted, it caused a great deal of resentment between us.'

Acceptance during your teenage years is so important in shaping your sense of self-worth. Geetha explains the importance from a teenagers' perspective: 'It's so very important because you're becoming a person, you're understanding who you are, and how people perceive you, and that perception is instrumental in your development. Nobody can be comfortable with who they are unless they have the acceptance of a larger group. If your personality is not accepted by friends, peers, and teachers, you are not confident that you are an attractive and likeable person who will develop into a functioning adult.'

And acceptance has to come from all the different groups that make up this complex tribal culture in a school. These classifications have come from the students themselves, always starting with one particular group. 'The cool group were social butterflies, and the rest of us didn't necessarily want to be like them, we saw they were always partying and their Instagram and Facebook posts were ideal—I didn't want to be that,' she says. But there are also the 'woke groups'—slang for socially aware and politically conscious groups—who come in for criticism because they see themselves as 'intellectuals' and are politically correct all the time. And finally the butt of several jokes are the 'nerds' and the 'jocks'. As a parent and educator, I hadn't realized how hard this phase of needing to be accepted was for our teens and their words were a revelation. This acceptance is yearned for at a number of different levels and right on top of the list of challenges is physical appearance.

Acceptance and pressure go hand in hand when it comes to how you look—our appearance is made up of several social and economic indicators. Indeed, what is the perfect 'look' in the eyes of our teens? Is there a pecking order of things you need to tick to gain that acceptance?

'Oh absolutely,' says Vanita. 'I think it's being attractive at that age. Slim, tall—in our class dark and fair didn't come to it. But that comes from families—I remember when I came from the UK once, having spent all my time in the sun, and I was seven shades darker than I am now, my mum opened the door and she gasped, "Maine to gora bacha paida kiya tha"'—I gave birth to a fair-skinned child!

'And yes, speaking English well, it's right up there in the hierarchy. Also, having confidence and being assured how well to do you were. And those girls and guys who could not speak up and take part in conversations, people didn't give a toss about them, they didn't even bother to try and reach out and talk to these people.'

I cannot even begin to imagine how stressful this must be. Every waking hour you need to be beautiful, glamorous, adored by fans, and most importantly, you need to be thin. Gayatri recounts her experiences of being more than a size zero! 'You definitely have to be thin. I've always been heavy, in my early teens, you would say, chubby. And I've been fat shamed—but that was a struggle and is still a struggle. I am dark skinned, I have curly hair, I am the opposite of what the idealized North Indian beauty would be—fair skin, straight hair, and thin, so that is the struggle. Popular kids were the girls who adhered to these standards.'

Gayatri got used to being picked on, and it started as early as the third grade. 'Oh you look different, you are heavy, and the struggle starts from there and it still continues. We keep getting exposed to this idealized beauty, in media, in films, so you don't understand the work that goes on behind it, this look is only possible after five to seven hours of make-up and fifteen hours of workouts and editing and photo shopping. This will always be a struggle.'

My heart went out to her. My own personal struggle with weight as a teenager, until I finally lost it at eighteen and then piled it on after the birth of my son, has been a long continuous journey of always feeling fat. I can't look at myself in the mirror even after losing kilos when I was diagnosed with diabetes, without seeing a fat person grimacing back at me. I wondered whether it made Gayatri unhappy and sure enough it did.

'Definitely. There are still days when I just feel ugly. Some days you just don't want to go outside. When you wear something and go outside, you want to run back in because you feel you're not looking your best self, and even your best self would never compare with someone else. That sort of pressure is very common. It's like a snowball rolling down a hill, it just keeps getting bigger and bigger and you don't know how to stop that momentum. It's affected my confidence, my self-esteem, and those are areas I have had to seriously work on.'

She confesses she was too lazy to do anything about her weight. But there were so many others who were indulging in anorexic and bulimic behaviours, and talking about what they put their bodies through, with pride. 'Hey I've been eating only celery for the past one week—and I've lost four kilos! There was always constant chatter on how to diet to lose weight, and sure enough, the moment they ate normal food they would double the weight, so then they would try and make it more extreme and just not eat at all! In their own eyes they were obese. This was very normal in school. Dieting was glorified and there were a lot of anorexics. I can remember some students would just eat two cucumbers for lunch.'

The way you look determines how popular you are, and worse still, whether your peers turn their noses up at you.

BANI SHARES HER STORY

'I was looked down upon because I was not conventionally attractive, and I was overweight and had braces and pimples at a time when everyone was going off into relationships, discovering puberty. I was mocked. So, people gave guys dares, "If you don't do this you're going to have to kiss the fat girl's hand." It was a very toxic environment, and that became a big part of how I viewed myself.

'I still do that today. I still have issues with the way I view myself and the seeds for that were sown really early on, right from school. And there were fat jokes. I remember a teacher, I don't know what she had against me, there was no AC remote in the class, and this was seventh grade, so I pulled up a chair and turned on the AC and as I jumped down, she said, "Oh my God girl, don't jump there's going to be an earthquake" in front of the whole class—so that reinforced that it was okay to make fat jokes, and it didn't matter that I had thyroid.

'It made me cry. By the time I went to university I was looking at myself as someone who people were going to do a favour by being with me. There were a lot of tough lessons to be learnt, until I believed I should not be underselling myself like that. Now, I've come to a place where I'm comfortable with myself. And that was due to a play I did much later in life, during my time at the University of Exeter, called *The Cabaret*. That whole process was therapeutic and cathartic, since we had to take our clothes off, and I thought, people are going to see me naked, and they're just going to have to deal with it, and if they don't like it—that's fine. But they all loved it. Because I loved doing it. If you approach something with confidence and not with shame they're going to respect that confidence.

'That was the confidence I was lacking through school. The shame was reinforced in gym class—you were always getting picked last for the teams, and nobody wanted you on their side because you were a liability. And once you're sidelined in sport, you're sidelined in the social groups, and you tend to be a part of a very small group that accepts you. But I am better at sieving those bits out now and I know that I'm happier now, and I'm fine.

'And so I stayed off social media. I posted nothing. I was terrified about what they would say, the remarks, and the comments. Boys and girls were both complicit. Outwardly, nobody said, don't sit with her because she's fat, but they were making jokes. I used to hate the height and weight checks at school—I remember all the boys would linger after they had done their checks just to see what my weight was. And I used to dread those days, and whenever I could I would not come to school.

'I'm always terrified of weighing myself, I haven't weighed myself for over a year now, that shame, related to that number on the scales, still haunts me. When people are laughing at you, you know that you're never going to be accepted. And it wasn't just me, I remember a boy, Shivam, having that same problem, it was all of us, we were really looked down upon for not looking a certain way.

'My release came when I was performing on stage, as a singer and as an actor. Because that was when I was appreciated, and it helped me get more comfortable in my skin, because I knew I was good, I was getting the validation and I really needed it at that time. Even the guys who made fun of me and called me fat, whenever I sang in front of an audience, they would come and tell me I had done a good job. How heavy I am doesn't determine how high I can sing! Thankfully! I didn't think about what was happening in class when I was on stage.'

Priya talks frankly about how looking a particular way did her head in. And interestingly how social media, which we blame for so many ills, also helped her feel more positive about herself.

'Seventh grade was also about the time when I was going through puberty and it's the time when you're gaining weight, growing taller, and to make matters worse, my teeth were all over the place. Everything is going through a change and you don't know how you fit in. I was getting acne at the same time, and you don't feel confident. Then you go to social media and you see these people with perfect skin and they're thin and they look like how beautiful people look. But, and here's the thing—the good thing was that on social media while a lot of people were really thin, you had a lot of fat people as well, who were putting out positive vibes encouraging body positivity.

'I didn't get a lot of positivity about my weight, since my family members would comment upon it. I'm okay with it now but earlier I was a lot more conscious about it. It made me unhappy and I became conscious about how fat my thighs were, I was conscious about the clothes I wore, and how they would fit me. I didn't stop eating but there were times I would skip a meal even though I was really hungry. But now when I feel hungry I eat, because it's not healthy. I am so much better now because on social media I have had examples of people who have stood up for the way they are and accepted themselves.'

For Damini it was the start of Instagram that drove her to lose weight. 'I did feel pressured since I was a very fat kid and people made fun of me in school. Instagram was coming up at that time and I decided I have to be on Instagram and for that I would have to get thin! My dada was also after me saying I was unhealthily fat and I had to lose weight—so I lost the weight. I regulated my diet, got a personal trainer, and swam every day.'

They all agreed that there was a huge amount of pressure on girls from a young age, from the way they looked, to the way they talked, every little piece had to be picture perfect. What was distressing was that in this list of indicators to be cool and beautiful, tall, thin, and well-spoken in English was added the element of colour. You needed to be fair.

Jayanti recounts the trials of being dark in a fair skin obsessed India. 'When I was younger, the idea of being dark in a country that worshipped fair skin was something that was projected on me. You had to be fair. This wasn't coming from my parents but from society. That's really hard to deal with while you're growing up because it causes so many issues later. You don't accept your body and the person that you are.'

This saddens me as I learn that girls begin to try lightening their faces using collagen, bleaching, and Botox. 'It makes no sense,' cries Priya, who is fair skinned herself. 'How does being fair change you? How does it make you special or unique? I can't begin to tell you what girls in my class try, other than all kinds of home remedies, including haldi and dahi…they shop for face lightening options from overseas. It is really absurd to hear it from my generation.'

And now with technology you can hide yourself away and present a very different picture of yourself on social media. Meena recounts the experience of her cousin:

'She has a beautiful dark face, clear skin, and she has to edit her face, making it several shades lighter, so that she gets likes on Instagram. That is just so sad that people are not able to appreciate the skin they're born with, the skin they're supposed to accept. Imagine the kind societal pressure that's making you edit yourself for the outside world. There's this one app called Beauty Plus and it allows you to whiten your face. Look at all the new actresses in Bollywood, they all look the same—they are all fair, there are no dark mainstream actresses.

The popular girls are all stick thin and fair. The saddest part is that because of social media people judge you on your appearance. There is a pressure on girls to put themselves out there as beautiful and perfect and alter themselves.'

Everyone seems to be on a perpetual diet, girls and boys, and everyone goes to the gym. I feel their pain and anxiety 24/7 at having to look perfect all the time. A young sixteen-year-old I know, on a school holiday, ensures she spends a couple of hours putting on full make-up, the whole nine yards—foundation, false eyelashes, highlighters, hair straighteners, before she spends the morning in bed on her phone so that she looks her best on FaceTime calls. There is a deep sense of unhappiness all the time about how they look—it made me wonder how they managed to get out of bed in the morning.

This pressure and obsession with looking a particular way—I wondered whether teenage boys felt the same pressures? Ravi was certain that it affected boys. 'I think they do, they just don't talk about it openly. That's what our society does, men don't talk about problems, ergo men don't have problems! You're supposed to be outgoing, talk to everyone, God forbid you're a shy guy and you find that difficult—the pressure is on you to take the initiative. And you need to be good at sports! I've experienced that, I have struggled with that for so long. In the popularity stakes, the sports jocks call the shots. I know of peers who actually use fairness creams for men.'

SMARTPHONES AND THE QUEST FOR VALIDATION

A teen and their phone are seldom parted, and their closest relationship appears to be with their phone. It's their comfort zone, security blanket, and their way of life. They live their life through social media. According to news reports, millennials spend one-third of their waking hours on their phones.[8]

The students that I spoke to were happy to share how their parents wrestle with the teens' screen time and social media usage. At sixteen, Amina has a calling curfew, she cannot call anyone after 11 p.m. Her mother tried to impose a texting curfew but she manages to get round that!

---

[8]'Indian millennials addicted to smartphones, spend one-third of their waking hours on WhatsApp, Facebook, *Economic Times*, 20 December 2019.

So what are they doing on their phones late at night when parents are fretting about their lack of sleep? Jatin spends his time chatting and watching Netflix since he does not have a TV in his room, and feels conventional TVs are redundant anyway. Jatin is hooked to streaming services. So how does he get round any phone curfews his parents may try and impose? He grins—'My dog is parked outside and when my mum's coming he barks so I can hide my phone. But hey she's very clever, and when I study, she wants to take my phone and keep it with her. So I have no option but to hand it over.'

Manvi ruefully shares the fact that she's not allowed to keep her phone with her at night because it disrupts her sleep cycle. 'We don't have TV, we watch Netflix on our phones, or our laptops. Conversations can last five to seven hours sometimes, starting at midnight till the small hours of the morning, or we FaceTime each other, once we actually slept while talking to each other!'

'You can't win against the phone,' says Garima emphatically. 'It's all down to social media. Parks are empty of kids, there are no kids, they're on their phones, computers, games, and it's an addiction. These games have combined the worst of two things—they have games and they've made them superficially social. So kids could be playing with some dude in Russia and now it's all social media gaming.'

Seema confesses, 'I used to be on my phone all the time, my dad would come home and I would be on a call with my friends and I realized that it's not right. He never said anything. I am a family person and I think it was a phase. If you use social media carefully it's not all bad. For me it's a break from my studies, I keep connected with my friends, and I'm not getting addicted. If you have the balance everything is okay but if you give it priority over everything else, then that's a big problem. My phone used to be my priority, but now I am putting my studies and family first.'

Kalyani has just signed up for a masters and it is interesting to see her perspective of her last years in school. 'I don't think you realize it as pressure until you're older. It gives you a lot of validation and it does give you a dopamine rush with likes, getting messages, and having a full inbox. And you don't realize the kind of effect it has on you and the kind of impact it has on the way you see yourself. It has a huge impact and it puts a lot of pressure but we don't realize that pressure till we're older. So looking back I can see how stereotypes travel faster on social media, in a lot of ways they really solidify what a girl should be, what a boy should be, and yeah they do try and make us conform to that idea.'

She tried to conform in her own way in the way she dressed and how she wanted to be photographed. 'We were following the trends of the TV shows we watched, following celebrities on Facebook, checking out what they wore, how they held themselves. And yes, we wanted to be like them. So you dress like Hannah Montana or whatever. That becomes a mantra—this is what a girl must look like, and there is not enough space for you to break out because everybody around you is also looking to that for reference. It gives you no space for your individuality, it keeps it dormant. You do grow out of it, though, a lot of people do.'

Students are joining Instagram and Snapchat towards the end of junior school now. So they are experiencing the dopamine rush that you get when you see the likes and the blue ticks, and which create both an envy and a longing for similarly happy, fuss-free times. Students spoke frankly about looking at their friends' pictures and wanting to travel to those places that they saw on the posts. They felt a huge pressure to have as many likes as possible and to have 'followers'. It wasn't enough to just be who they were, they needed the followers. And there is a new definition of 'cool' on Instagram—if you follow less than half of your followers, then you're cool. And as soon as you get to a thousand followers, you're up there!

This relentless quest for likes is killing all our fun, according to journalist Josh Glancy, who writes a weekly column for the *Sunday Times Magazine*. Instagram, he says, has become a hazardous pastime. And he gives a few disturbing instances.

'Instagrammability,' writes Glancy, 'has already seeped into millennials' decision making, affecting what holiday they decide to go on, or which dish they choose to order at a restaurant where the camera now eats first. This is destroying our capacity to live in the moment, and it is joyless. The more Instagrammable something is, the less memorable it turns out to be. Everything is captured, nothing is worthwhile.'

I have to confess I agree. Nothing gets me going more than having to stop for that Instagram moment. I have a dear friend who will not let anyone eat unless she has clicked pictures of the food on the dining table, whether it's a plate of fried eggs or an ordinary go-to homemade salad.

Malini, who was introduced to social media when she was twelve years old, confesses, 'You want to be on it, because your friends are on it, and you want to be accepted, and that was a pressure I faced on Snapchat. You feel the need to show people where you are, it's not about memories. I feel it's become a part of society that everyone needs to be a part of, otherwise you don't feel accepted.' She loses track of time when she's on social media, and scrolling through Instagram, she clocks in four to six hours of screen time a day—a figure that is shocking even to her.

Jasmeet concurs—'There is this pressure to look a certain way and to be a certain way. Social media shows the best parts of everyone's life. So it was always this fear of missing out FOMO. There's a pic of this person on the beach splashing in the water and having fun, and my response is, "Oh I wish I could do that", or there are a group of friends having fun at a party and I think, "Oh I wish my friends and I could have fun like that". You feel that by sitting in your room you're missing out on a lot of stuff that life has for you and at the same time you don't want to leave this room where you're scrolling through countless people's lives. And you end up feeling you're not as good as everyone else, or your life is not as exciting as everyone else's.'

What a terribly distressing way to view your life. Did it make her attempt to make her life as interesting as the idealized ones she saw? She shrugs, and answers, 'No. I think I was too lazy to take the plunge. I just went into this self-pity mode. I would just use that to make myself feel worse. Only over this past year have I come to the realization that I need to be more present in what I'm doing and enjoy my life with the specific people I love, but that is very recent.'

And she is not alone. Malini accepts it has made her very lazy too. 'I'm just lying on my bed, I don't feel like doing anything because I have everything on my device, my earphones, I can watch movies for hours, I don't need anything else. I live by proxy.' Those words—'I live by proxy'—stayed with me. What does it do to young people when they can't own their own narrative?

Madhumita Ramakrishnan, psychologist and presently a PhD scholar, has been researching the effects of technology across the economic spectrum. She is concerned about the information overload that teens from across all walks of life are assailed by. 'These platforms have blurred all cultural boundaries. They believe that their lives are not complete without the experiences of dating and proms. There is also a complete blurring of right and wrong. There is absolutely no moral compass in many cases. They have so much information and everybody is showcasing their perspective.'

We need to keep in mind that the adolescent brain is still developing and is very susceptible to influences and perspectives. She recounts how the teens in her class responded to the show *You* when it was released. 'In the show a guy is stalking a girl and he kills off her friend because she caught on to him, and it was really popular amongst the children because they saw it as a pursuit for relentless love, and in their book that was so romantic for them. There is no filter to counter the information onslaught. They don't know—because they know too much.'

Madhumita is just eight years older than her senior students and enjoys a strong connect with the teens she teaches. She shared glimpses of her own school years to give them an experience of a life when social media didn't exist. Her students were aghast! A life without social media...they truly felt she had led a deprived life. What was striking in this conversation was how our students' social fabric had undergone a monumental change in under a decade, and according to the psychologist Madhumita it's all down to the toxicity of social media.

'They don't realize the toxicity that they're exposed to which we were safely kept away from. I'm not just talking about networking sites like Instagram and Snapchat—you also have all the streaming channels. They need to detox. They're in a constant state of being overwhelmed—they say I don't know what to do, everybody is doing so much. My heart goes out to them.'

Her research is on behavioural issues in children. She has been talking to parents, teachers, and students from both lower and higher ends of the economic spectrum. And across the board there is a unanimous opinion that there is no interaction in the family any more. 'This is not just a problem of privilege. I'm talking to families of chauffeurs and house helps. These parents are struggling to give their children the cell phones and devices they want—they are anguished because they can't provide this and they don't want their kids to feel deprived because they are doing everything they can to give them a better economic future.'

Clearly, at both ends of the spectrum, parents are working hard to provide their children with a quality of life, which often means they don't have the time. And when they do get together, everybody is leaning down into their phones, and the gulf between the children and parents keeps on widening. Children feel that parents don't understand the pressures they feel, and the parent feels they are on the outside of their microcosm. There is alienation at both ends.

Sapna is a senior and experienced teacher who has been a guidance counsellor and has both mentored and been a confidante to many teenagers. What saddens her is how young lives are being eroded by a sense of low self-worth. 'Most of these kids are very bright kids yet all of them think they're not good enough. I keep telling them that they should decide what is cool, but again it is their need for acceptance, and at this stage in their lives they want this acceptance above all else.'

Acceptance, belonging, fitting in, it keeps coming back to that, and if you feel outside the circle then you feel alone. BBC Radio 4 carried out a nationwide survey in 2018, the largest of its kind in the UK. Its results are revealing. Forty per cent of the respondents in sixteen to twenty-four years of age said they feel lonely very often as compared to 29 per cent in sixty-five to seventy-four years of age. The study was carried out by academics at the Universities of Manchester, Exeter, and Brunel (London). It assessed 55,000 people aged sixteen and over and found that those who report feeling the loneliest tended to have more 'online relationships'. The five main characteristics of being lonely according to the survey are: having nobody to talk to, feeling disconnected from the world, feeling left out, sadness, and not feeling understood. Interestingly, women feel more shame about feeling lonely than men.[9] So while they are crowded with the information and online relationships, don't they miss human contact? Is a virtual life a substitute for a real one?

Ravi's response is matter-of-fact. 'It's become a way of life, our lifestyle is so different from our parents. We come home and check our phones, that's the first thing you check, it's a natural instinct, so even when I don't have my phone on me (in school), I find myself checking my pockets, I'm so used to having this lifeline. I cannot imagine life without a phone.'

So what do they get out of it? What's the joy?

'When you think about it, there's no joy. It's time wasting, consuming, my daily screen time is around five hours—for instance I slept at 5 a.m. this morning because I was on my phone.'

---

[9] '16-24 year olds are the loneliest age group according to new BBC Radio 4 survey', BBC, 1 October 2018.

Shaming, trolling, call it what you will, is another form of bullying and we have grown to accept cyberbullying as a given. The digital world takes the eternal issue of bullying and turns it into something pervasive. This bullying is not face to face. The victim's sorrow does not affect the empathy of the bully precisely because it's not face to face. It's a different kind of communication where it is easy to be cruel. It's like the term 'collateral damage' during a war. The consequences of the action are not really thought through in the same way.

Sadly, girls seem to be more susceptible and this in turn drives low self-worth. With the creation of WhatsApp groups and Instagram, this unkindness and downright cruelty has escalated. Sapna shares her anguish as a teacher. 'These WhatsApp groups play a very negative role. They joke with each other but these jokes have become very mean—they call it dark humour. There are comments on the way people look—they are openly rejected, pronounced as failures—and the person at the receiving end is just supposed to laugh and take it. And everybody is apparently doing it. What is it about making someone feel miserable that is amusing to those who do it? I spoke to my students about this kind of cruel laughter and urged them to think about such things. It's a kind of mob mentality. It bothers everyone but people remain complicit because nobody wants to be the odd one out. It's such a sad vicious circle.'

A leading principal from a Mumbai school makes it a point to speak to the students at assemblies on this particular topic. Her poignant question always is—why can't we all be kinder to each other? They know what she is saying, they agree with what she is urging them to do, but she says they don't appear to have the strength to stand out in a crowd. It's an epidemic and it's getting worse. Kindness and compassion appears to be a kind of weakness.

Tarini agrees. 'Kindness can be seen as a vulnerability, and if confidence is prioritized when it comes to popularity, then vulnerability is not something that people will want to show. We are always encouraged to be tough, to be competitive, and to be the first, top of the line, top of the heap. We aren't encouraged to be kind and compassionate.' But surely, I counter, we receive many little kindnesses every day of our lives, and so don't we learn from that?

'Maybe,' says Sapna. 'Or maybe in some warped way—the world that we are in and all the messages they are getting are telling them that these are unimportant things, these are insignificant things, and you need to be tougher, you need to be more strident, you need to be aggressive, because that's what they see on social media, violence and aggression and the complete lack of compassion. I keep telling them that so many of you love animals, and are part of groups seeking kindness for animals—where does that compassion go when it comes to compassion for other human beings? Particularly your peers?'

When I shared this with the students, they ruefully concurred. Dhruti talked about an account called 'School Secrets' where 'They write stuff that is going on with several students, and these are eighth graders. Like *Gossip Girl* [a hit American TV series very popular with teenagers] it was mainly gossip, and they were writing a lot of hurtful stuff that affected a lot of people.'

Ameeta shared a post with me while we were in the midst of our conversation. A young girl no more than fourteen was posting pictures of herself in short dresses from different angles. My heart went out to her. What I saw was a vulnerable young girl, desperate to be part of the cool group, yearning to be 'liked' and validated. In response, what she got was a vicious post from a schoolmate that derisively made fun of her attempt and included cruel swear words. Why? Where is this coming from?

Tarini attempted to explain. 'A lot of people in our grade want to be really funny because it makes them appear cool, so they think the best way is to mock people. They use their confidence and humour to joke about someone, put them down, and the rest of us laugh, no matter how awful that joke was. Everybody is so contained, they don't look outside themselves, and image is all there is and it's defined by your presence on social media.'

She took the decision to stay away from Instagram and posting. 'I'm not on Instagram. I don't want to be part of it. It comes from a strange kind of judgement. Girls bringing down girls. It's called slut-shaming, it's easier to post it and it wrecks so many people, they troll the way the girls dress and shame them. I wouldn't know what to do if someone said that about me.'

As parents and teachers, we have to help children understand this. Like Tarini, they have the option to opt out and yet have a fulfilling life. Also, more attention needs to be paid to the role of the bystander since the circulation is so fast. They need to understand the words of Elie Wiesel, author, Nobel laureate, and Holocaust survivor, 'What hurts the victim most is not the cruelty of the oppressor, but the silence of the bystander.' Children need to be sensitive to the harm caused by social media. With digital technology there is no time to think through the consequences of any action, the damage is immediate and often irreversible—everything lives on forever on the internet. Parents and teachers need to focus on this and the risks this involves. Discussions and dialogues with young people which ask them to consider laying down moral codes are necessary. We need to get them to consider what responsible behaviour in such situations is, and above all, focus on developing empathy in our children.

A IS FOR ANXIETY: GENERATION ANXIOUS

Anxiety is spreading like an epidemic. An estimated one in seven Indians suffered from mental disorders of varying severity in 2017 with depression and anxiety being the commonest, according to a study published in the Lancet Psychiatry.[10] According to a report by the leading mental health and neuroscience centre NIMHANS Bangalore, almost one out of five adolescents suffers from some level of mental morbidity. 'Children get more overwhelmed now with

---

[10]PTI, 'Mental disorder cases doubled in less than 3 decades, anxiety and depression most common condition', *Economic Times*, 24 December 2019.

disruptions in their life than they did earlier.[11] Panic attacks have become very common in school children. There has been a rise in the number of cases related to body shaming as well. Children are increasingly involved in activities where they sit at home, instead of playing physically, or are involved in performance sports at all times,' says Parimal Pandit, the project director of a counselling and assessment department in a school for people with special needs.[12]

Why? What is happening in the lives of our children that is adding to their anxiety? Reality television, social media, academic pressures, or conflict at home? Are children more anxious now, or are we as parents passing on our own fears and worries and becoming more eager to get them diagnosed? What is this anxiety that paralyses children, debilitates them, stops them from going to school, and how is this different from children feeling nervous about things? Clearly having butterflies in your tummy before a performance is not the same.

Before wading in with specialists and statistics I thought it was important to hear the voices of the teens, educators, and parents who are grappling with this major concern.

Parineeta believes the pressures she feels at sixteen cannot be understood by her seniors. 'Everything is making us anxious. Academic achievement is topmost but I find social anxiety the most problematic. It's hard for me. If I'm going to a party, I start thinking about it a few days in advance, what will I say if I don't know anyone there, I find it hard to make conversation. I don't like to go anywhere without my core group of friends. That for me is a problem. Anxiety is something that everyone faces, everyone that I know gets very anxious about certain things and that's only natural.'

Manvi is conscious of the stigma she faced when she started going to a therapist. 'Some people treat going to therapy as a disease! I was really confused myself, anxious about whether my signs were

---

[11]Aditya Mani Jha and Payel Majumdar Upreti, 'Teens and trauma', *Hindu BusinessLine*, 21 July 2019.
[12]Ibid.

depressive. My sister had been diagnosed with depression in her early teens and had needed hospitalization. I kept wondering whether I was going the same way, and there was no one to talk to.'

Prerna took the route of going to the school counsellor in the eighth grade because she was being bullied. 'I used to have long periods lasting for two weeks sometimes and the backache was unbearable and I needed to lie down in the infirmary. So the boys began to make fun of me—I was called a sicko! It got worse when the main bully started crushing paper balls and chucking them at me, calling me trash, calling me fat, and many other boys followed him. I would come home crying every single day. It was so hurtful.'

Tarini agrees that 'Mental health is an issue—but so many girls just put stuff out there about their depression, anxiety, and panic attacks, you just don't know who genuinely needs help. There's a difference between being sad and clinically depressed. You can be anxious about exams in twelfth grade, but does that count as a condition with physiological manifestations? I'm in an environment where people casually say they have mental health problems, and that's a problem. This girl in ninth grade dumped so much emotional baggage on me. I think she did it for attention. I don't know what's true and what's not with mental health. Guys and girls both do this.'

Psychologist and teacher Madhumita agrees that whilst earlier students would refer to themselves as being worried, or stressed, now they've started using the term anxiety. More students have started consulting school counsellors as well as therapists outside of school. Perhaps this is because children are never taught emotional intelligence, neither at home nor at school, and in an increasingly digital world, they are often unable to manage the intensity of their emotions or understand them.

'I hate to put a dampener on this,' she says, 'but there's appears to be a romanticizing of mental illness. There is nothing called "worried" any more, it is anxiety, and their moodiness is bipolarity. They are exposed to so much and there is nobody telling them where the boundary lies, where the cut-off is. They go on about hyperventilating, having panic attacks. No, you're not, you're worried and your heart rate is escalating and that happens when you're nervous but you're not having a panic attack. And when parents are not equally informed it gets reinforced. "Oh my God what's happening to my child! My child read about this on Google." So as a psychologist, as a teacher who has taught for several years, my constant worry is—stakeholders are not informed enough.'

This is reflected in what Dr Parmar sees as an escalation in the numbers of parents seeking help for what they see as their child's anxiety. 'The world for these kids is so much about image, even something like going to a psychiatrist or therapist is cool. It's cool and they have to go to the best. They ask each other, "Who is your therapist...mine is so and so"—it sometimes renders me speechless when I hear these things. They don't like to go to the school counsellor since it means going during school and in full view of their peers. I feel they must be feeling so trapped in all these layers of having to be.'

This doesn't take away from the facts before us. According to the latest National Crime Records Bureau data, India recorded a new high of 12,526 suicides by students. The percentage has sharply risen by 21.19 per cent since 2019. The data collected since 1995 reveals that more than 1.8 lakh students have committed suicide, of which the year 2020 recorded the highest number.[13] Taking their own lives is the final step, but there are signs that as parents and educators we need to be aware of and pick up on. I am referring specifically to self-harm.

SELF-INJURY/SELF HARM

I cannot remember when the spectre of what is now termed as self-injury and self-harm raised itself in schools. I know that as educators

---

[13]Simran Sharma, 'Student Suicides On An All Time High, Warns NCRB Data,' *Logical Indian*, 18 January 2022.

it caught us completely unawares and it took a while for counsellors, parents, and schools to begin to work out ways of addressing it. I believe that this too has escalated in the last ten years, and it was confirmed by students in my conversations with them.

Gayatri graduated four years ago and relates how common it was in her class with several students who would cut themselves, sometimes they did it because it was the 'in' thing to do, and influenced no doubt by what they viewed on TV. 'There was this TV show, a teen drama called *Skins* in which a lot of us were introduced to this world of self-harm and mental health issues. A lot of people started self-harming, wondering, does it actually help my feelings, and then it's a kind of addiction. When you're feeling bad, you cut, and it distracts you—the pain takes over, and you're caught in a cycle. It becomes a cycle that you use to deal with your problems. Then someone sees a friend doing that and thinks, "Yeah, maybe this could help me feel better", and it becomes like a domino effect. But it wasn't as rampant as it is now.'

Tanya in the eleventh grade confirms how common cutting is amongst her peers. 'For instance, there was our friend who cut himself because his girlfriend of five days was sad about something! Of course, we yelled at him something rotten and told him to stop doing it for the drama and attention. This is a new low. Another girl used a cutter from the art room after a fight with her boyfriend. Another cut her arms—she was pretending to hide it but wanted to be found—for attention from her peers.'

But it's not always about seeking attention. Maina shared she had cut herself when she was feeling low. Her mother, who is a psychologist, diagnosed her anxiety as being school related and helped her change her school. 'I was lucky that my mother understood, because family pressures can trigger an anxiety attack. Say someone needs a really good grade and then doesn't get it. A panic attack follows, they can't breathe, and they have to stand under a shower to calm themselves down. These instances happen. I know of seven kids from class who used to cut themselves, sometimes over a break-up and because they believed life wasn't worth living—but now it's not a trend. Now if someone has depression and anxiety we treat it as serious in school.'

Damini, too, cut herself in the eighth grade and shares what drove her to that point. 'I had so much going on at school. I wasn't doing well and my parents were coming down really harshly on me because of that. And there were family issues, and issues with friends, there was too much to handle. I didn't know what to do, so I just did it. I cut myself on my arms when I was by myself, at home, and my friends saw the cuts and they shared it with a teacher. My parents were called to school. They made them sign an agreement that said that if your child harms themselves in school it is not the school's responsibility. So instead of counselling the parents and talking to me, I got shouted at by my dad, "Why are you doing these things", and I said "Dude, just understand the problem."'

In her father's defence, as an adult of another generation, he would find this act incomprehensible. So what was going on in her mind when she started harming herself?

'I just couldn't cope with what was going on. My parents were separated for a year, my brother left for college. I did it because I didn't know what else to do,' she says. The good news is she found a healer she could connect with and who brought positivity into her life. She doesn't feel the urge or need to harm herself now. But she hasn't forgiven her parents for not taking her despair seriously, because everybody needs a go-to person and often friends alone cannot help.

Deepa is very concerned that so many students are going through this. 'There was this really nice guy in eighth grade, we saw his hands and we asked him, "What are you doing, why are doing this stuff?" So we took him to the counsellor. I was so disgusted when the school did nothing to help. I look at some of my peers and see that their hands are full of cuts, up till their elbows, and they have to wear full sleeves even in the height of summer. It's more with girls but it's clinically proven that girls at this age are more prone to self-harming themselves. Perhaps it's the amount of pressure that is put on girls at such a young age, from the way we look, to the way we talk, every little thing has to be ideal and perfect.'

Clearly, as parents and educators, we now need to understand and empathize with what drives our young people to harm themselves. As a psychologist, Madhumita has had to remind parents to be watchful about their teens' behaviour. 'Parents have to look out for the child. Why is your child wearing a full-sleeved T-shirt in summer? Why is she only eating salad? Observe and understand. It could be an eating disorder, a condition that has risen so sharply these last seven years. Boys and girls are overworking themselves in gyms and not eating enough because they want to look a particular way. This entire six-pack culture is a pressure on our kids. I have met my share of boys who remodel themselves to be attractive to girls. So now, guys want to be sports heroes as well as intellectuals, and be sensitive and good looking! It's unrealistic. And when you don't succeed, you feel bad about yourself, which hurts, so you cut yourself believing it will distract you and relieve the pain.'

I asked a group of drama students to write about their personal experiences of self-harm, this is what a fourteen-year-old had to say:

> At first, it's nothing,
> just ignoring the feeling of something,
> you start to think, you stop and wonder,
> how you got yourself into this mighty blunder,
> the blood of the slits,
> dripping from your wrists,
> leaves you more satisfied,
> than the time you hid and cried,
> you feel like you're locked away,
> there's no escape, you're forced to stay,
> you ponder on how it's made such an impression,
> this room of hell you're locked in is depression.

As educators, we have to be watchful for signs and be there to help. Take the instance of Kirat, eighteen years old, in his last year at school and clearly a bright, sensitive, and ethical young man who just broke down during a tutorial with his tutor. Sonali, his tutor, was distressed and dismayed: 'He's not the kind of kid who does that. I felt it's emotional abuse over years and he was cutting himself because he desperately needed his parents' attention. He wanted to do well so that he would get the kind of attention he needed. He trusted me enough to talk to me, and he said, "Ma'am I've got cuts and my parents, especially my mum, just does not notice me. I have cuts on my arms and I sit in my T-shirt next to her and she's never noticed." I asked him if he had stopped, since she is not noticing his injuries. He said, "I have not been able to stop"—he showed me the cuts—he had used a blade.'

On her recommendation, he started seeing a therapist but his parents were in denial and they stopped the sessions as well as the prescribed antidepressants. The reason? They believed the medication would make him drowsy and would impact his studies. His tutor was unable to persuade them otherwise. 'He has had a lot of rejections from Ivy League institutions, but he got into some good colleges. He's such a good hearted person! It just breaks my heart.'

Heartbreaking it certainly is—I think back to the kinder, gentler times that I grew up in and indeed even the last decade of the 1990s and the early years of the turn of this century. Alongside the mental health concerns, our teens are young adults who are growing older younger and faster, beset by earlier onsets of all matters sexual. So what are the flashpoints when it comes to sexual activity? And what are the digital consequences of the pressure to put themselves out there?

FLASHPOINTS: SEXUALITY, PORNOGRAPHY, AND SUBSTANCE ABUSE

Interestingly, there is an acceptance of casual sex and a complete reliance on getting information and guidance about matters sexual from the internet. Teens I spoke to were well informed about protected sex and depended on the internet for 100 per cent of the information, but it did warp their expectations about the sexual experience.

'We got the net when we hit puberty and we have learnt everything on the net, and it was quite misleading. And we presumed this is how it goes. Discussions around pornography feature amongst girls and boys but within the boys it was more vocal, whereas amongst girls we tended to talk privately. There were plenty of us who thought this was how the real world works and then they were disillusioned, realizing it was all acting and totally scripted,' muses Gauri, wryly.

Manvi concurs—'I feel we get the wrong idea about sex. Pornography fantasizes it. You think it's all going to be smooth sailing and it's supposed to be so pleasurable—this is how you have to do it, and these are the noises you have to make. Your skin has to be smooth, your body has to be white and perfect.'

The bar for watching porn has also been lowered. Moyna relates that 'Sixth graders and even younger children are watching porn. Middle school is when you start looking at stuff, for guys it's like a topic of conversation. "Dude, I watched this last night", so you try it, and go, "Oh man what's that!" Then you're hooked. I think everybody believes that girls don't watch that much, but it also starts at the same age. But definitely the number of guys watching porn is greater.'

I wonder, are they able to speak to their parents about pornography? And there is a burst of laughter amongst the group that has gathered to talk about this topic. Diya is first off the mark, 'Heck no, I can't even talk to them about my periods! Some people are addicted, watching porn every day, especially guys, and it's also accepted that you have to watch. They don't expect girls to watch.'

Sexual experiences start in some cases around fifteen years of age, and the group educated me about the different bases! First base is kissing, second is French kissing, third is groping and taking off some clothes, and full blown sex is fourth base. Being in a relationship is desirable, so in that sense there is a pressure.

Maina looks back. 'For our grade it started when we were nine or ten. There's the cool group of people—they were sporty, good looking, and rich. They had big houses, big cars, shopping in London's Regent Street, shopping in Dubai. Delhi is just not good enough, they don't like the Delhi Zara! These were the cool people and they started dating in class five and six. So dating at that age was, "Shall we take a walk along the pool?" Now it's changed. Seventh grade is now quite intense and it's happening earlier. First base starts in class four or five.'

As parents, we need to set the template for healthy sexual relationships and as schools we need to inform our students about what consenting relationships mean. Coming from an unconventional family, where her understanding of a sexual relationship was really skewed led Veena to be lured into a harmful relationship with her tutor outside of school, a much older man.

She struggled to express herself as she shared her experience, when at fifteen, she became involved with her thirty-year-old teacher. 'It was a very toxic situation. I now realize that he was a paedophile, and that he took advantage of the fact that I didn't know what I was doing. I had come from a very troubled background at home. I was vulnerable and he took complete advantage of that, and when I tried to end it, he would stalk me. When I came to school, I would see his car parked outside and it was terrifying. I couldn't tell anyone. My friends knew and they were urging me to walk away, do something. I confessed to another guy on the course and he helped me. To this day I am so thankful to him because he literally saved me from that man. He went to the centre with the cops. I pulled out of the course. I could not tell my parents because I would have been banned from going out ever again. Now when I think about it, it was clearly sexual abuse, and it was not good and if I had understood consent and sexuality better I would have never got into that situation.'

Her trauma should ring warning bells for us adults. As parents, educators, and schools we need to teach our children about sexuality. I know it is hard for parents to do this alone, both tweens and teens are reluctant to have conversations with their parents at this stage, so this is where schools need to step in and create safe spaces for discussion and dialogue on these critical issues.

Veena found that the experience of abuse impacted the way she approached sex and her relationships as she got older. It was only when she went into therapy at university that her understanding grew. 'It was a stain, a scar, a wound that festers, and that coupled with the self-image issues I already had—it reinforced it and both things put together makes for a very risky combination. I realized that this was not the person I wanted to be, this was not the person I wanted to grow into, so I had to fix it, and I'm still fixing it, so yeah.'

Is there a pressure on girls to have sex if they are in a relationship? Are they aware of the need for consent, protected sex, and are they taking the necessary precautions?

Moyna believes that many end up doing it. 'It starts off as curiosity, then pressure, then thinking—why not? I think boys our age don't pressure the girls so much if the girl says I don't want to. But I've heard of cases where the girl has felt the pressure to give oral sex for the relationship to continue. What I'm uncomfortable about is that because it's a taboo, because our parents are not okay with our being sexually active at this age, children sneak around. If parents understand and accept that this is going to happen, we might as well make sure that the children understand protected sex, and that they aren't hiring shady rooms in random hotels and having sex. Some girls are on the pill, some girls have PCOS—polycystic ovary syndrome—so they have to be on the pill. But for others, you're dependent on the guy to ensure he has condoms.'

Kamini agreed that it's mostly protected sex, 'But a lot of my friends have had pregnancy scares and have had to get abortions done, stealing money from their parents to do it, trying chemical abortions that go wrong and mess up their cycles when they're fourteen. It's very young to be doing this kind of thing and they're not talking about this at home so they don't know that protection is something that has to be used.'

For several years, psychologist and teacher Madhumita has seen the changing attitudes to sexuality and the increasing pressure on girls: 'Asking for nudes, naked pictures, from any girl is much more widespread and is a form of cyberbullying. You ask for nudes, and then those nudes get circulated and there are stories of boys who are earning off it, money changes hands, and these are ninth graders I am referring to. I've heard of students being caught in classrooms, giving and receiving oral sex and going all the way. This may be happening in other countries, but in this society it is going to be received very differently. Here if you're caught, your parents are going to make you feel like crap for doing this. There is no, "Oh I understand you have hormones, you have needs". There is no space for that to be accepted over here.'

True to our patriarchal conditioning, teachers unfortunately tend to slut-shame the girls and there is never any conversation with the boy. 'It's about "her" morals, it's about how available "she" is. And that same conversation you have with the child comes back to the staff room, and then the child gets to hear of it,' she remarks sadly.

As educators there are some critical questions we have to ask ourselves. Do we have any jurisdiction over what our students do outside of schools? Often teachers get to know about all their social activity since they post pictures on social media. What is our role as educators at that point? Do we police our students? Do we report the information to the authorities? Or should we be reaching out to the student, open a channel of communication, and provide guidance and support? Clearly, in some instances, where groups indulge in shaming, bullying, and harassment, we cannot be silent. But when individual students appear to be losing their way and need an adult to help them think on the consequences of their revelations on digital platforms, we need to intervene as educators invested in our students' safety and well-being.

This level of sexual activity is not exclusive to students in privileged schools alone. It is present in government schools as well. In a conversation with government school teachers in a small town in Chennai, as part of her ongoing research, Madhumita was informed that their greatest challenge was teenage pregnancy. They tried segregating the students, different classrooms for girls and boys, in the hope that would deter them. The teachers found that the concept of repression in lower-income communities was higher. There was no space for discussion around sexual matters, and let's face it, teens are curious and very open to experimentation at this stage. Living in confined spaces, they are privy to the intimacies of adults, and sometimes it leads to angst or aggression, and sometimes it leads to just plain curiosity to try the same. It's all around them, on the internet pornography is rampant—all they need to do is to look for a channel.

At schools there is no platform for discussing sexuality. Organizations like TARSHI (Talking About Reproductive and Sexual Health Issues), a not-for-profit organization, is doing commendable work but so much depends on the teacher in the class to be able to take the conversation forward, and that just does not happen. Students cannot openly ask questions about contraception, pills, oral sex, abortion, and reproductive health. There is no information or conversation around these issues and they want to know more.

There are instances where a child has missed a period. She does not know who to talk to and it turns out she is pregnant. At this point suicidal tendencies and self-harm are the only things that come to mind. They know their parents are not going to accept it and they're going to be shamed. Who are they going to talk to? Who are they going to trust? Friends cannot guide you at such times. And counsellors find themselves trapped between the law and the need to help the child. 'There are very few schools where a counsellor can take care of the situation. Because [with the student being a minor] you are obligated to inform the parent. You inform the parent and there's a whole third degree that the child is going to go through. So how do you help?' asks Madhumita, helplessly.

From the conversations, it was evident that boys felt the pressure too, but it was more of boasting about their conquests. According to Aman, 'When you're hanging around and four out of the five guys are talking about what they've enjoyed sexually, you feel, "Yeah if they're doing it, I should be too". Also, it's the age factor, once you're eighteen, and if you haven't had sex, it's kind of sad. No one says it to your face, but you feel that's what they're thinking.'

Across the board young teens still struggle to find the space to talk about sexuality at home. Priya is certain that 'There is no conversation about sex in homes and schools hesitate to educate you about sex because they believe it will encourage you to have sex, and that is rubbish! We have no knowledge or understanding about consent and relationships.'

Tarini felt there was more pressure on girls. 'Girls are under pressure to put out. If there is a girl who has many sexual partners then she is a slut. If it's a guy who does that then he's a playboy and that's cool. It's just hypocrisy. By and large teens have protected sex, and my parents have talked to me about both sex and protection. Along with my friends we discovered that weird as it may sound *Cosmopolitan* on Snapchat has really good sex education! We have learnt a lot of important stuff about protection and what happens with your periods. We skip the sex positions page because we don't need it. It tells you about STDs as well, so thank you, *Cosmo*!'

She continues with a passionate plea: 'Why don't we have sex education? It's ridiculous, there is so much sexual activity but no sex-education class. No one wants to acknowledge the fact that it's happening. There is no point when hormones are raging to tell students—no sex. Instead, how about helping them—what is protected sex? How can you say no to someone who demands sex? We need to understand the need for consent.'

In its limited way her school attempted to educate the students on pornography. 'It was a joke,' she says angrily. The workshop leader was a man and he said, 'I also have watched porn, but it causes domestic rape. All of us were outraged!'

Kamini raises an important point about the conversation around sex in schools being largely heteronormative. 'When we learn about anything, whether it's about our own bodies, and this started off in sixth grade or so, they told us, "Your body is a temple", you must not defile it, you must not let a man touch you. But, and here's the thing—it's not always a man who is going to touch you if you're a woman! So I don't know what they educated us about.'

Vani agrees. 'If sex education focuses on heterosexual sex, it affects people who are gay or lesbian so badly. It's like the prejudice that was rampant when AIDS first hit the headlines, they called it the GRID—Gay-Related Infectious Disease. They pushed it as a representation of the gay community. They should have been teaching safe sex. You're pushing a whole group of people out by assuming they're all straight, and other assumptions include that everybody has a happy home and everybody will excel in school. And there is no one you can go to talk to! We were lucky we found a few teachers whom we could confide in, and could trust that it wouldn't become the talking point of staffroom gossip, or worse, that our parents would be called in. Discourse has always been a problem and it seems to be getting worse. Teachers don't seem to be listening to students.'

SUBSTANCE ABUSE

In the early to mid 1990s, cigarettes and alcohol were the main concerns of teachers and parents. By the late 1990s and early 2000s, cocaine and ecstasy were doing the rounds, while weed/hashish was always easily available. In the last decade, young teens are drinking sooner and harder. The norm appears to be to 'get wasted'. Many don't really enjoy the experience of the drink but wait for the effect that it has, and the same could be said for drugs that are available now.

Smoking around grades six, seven, or eight is becoming quite common and by the ninth grade, drinking is an acceptable social activity. 'If you were chilling after school, it would mean drinking, but people didn't use it as a crutch,' says Geetha. 'Plenty of us were smoking very young. You associate nicotine with problem relief and there was some shroom stuff going on. Parents know these house parties are going on where alcohol is present, and everyone there is underage. In some case parents provide the alcohol! My mother is against all this drinking and smoking thing. My parents don't like to talk about serious things, and they will hope to God that I will do the right thing—with other parents it's clearly different, when it comes to alcohol, parents let it go.'

Maina agrees that drinking is starting earlier now. 'Alcohol is very prevalent and starts depending on the group you're in. Seventh grade is the lower bar for cool people, for others it's the tenth grade; going to parties and drinking is very common for grades ten, eleven, and twelve. Some parents are okay with it at sixteen, others are a little more conservative. Beer is largely the drink of choice because it is cheap, or whisky, but typically it is vodka and shots. And it's not diluted, it's neat from the bottle! The thing is most teens start by drinking with friends. They have drivers who buy their alcohol for them.'

They spoke in a matter-of-fact manner about e-cigarettes being very common. Many sixth graders start experimenting with Jules. Hash is not considered to be a drug in the eyes of our teens and hash brownies on school trips are part of the experience of living in tents! Several have tried hash when they were fourteen years old, but interestingly, they draw the line at cocaine and MDMA, and are aware that these are hard drugs and they can be harmful. However, there are several who go off track and need rehabilitation. Sadly, some of their peers also have to drop out of school and pause their lives.

In the absence of verifiable statistics, is it really a problem? Experienced teachers seem to think that 80 per cent of teens in this age group are drinking and at least 55 per cent are on a variety of drugs. 'It's also getting easier to procure the drugs,' says Seema. 'There's home delivery for everything! Amongst my students there is fair amount of smoking up, and its de rigueur. The students know exactly where to go to—you go to Hanuman Mandir in Connaught Place and certain schools have these guys hanging around where you get it easily. So you can get ecstasy and Jules fairly easily.'

So how can schools help? According to Seema, 'Schools keep having talks for both parents and students. A lot of parents are in denial that this is happening to their child. It makes them uncomfortable. It also scares a lot of them. So we brought in an organization called Empower that works especially with this age group. The feedback was that after the session with the parents, many of them got appointments for help and counselling, which is good.'

So clearly, institutions need to create more spaces and platforms for discussions that are free flowing on all matters related to growing up, be it sexuality, pornography, substance abuse, and mental health. How do we create safe spaces within the school environment for these conversations is a critical area and we'll discuss that more in our next chapter.

ACCEPTANCE AND ENGAGEMENT

Whilst being focused on their personal lives and challenges, it is at this stage that our teens begin to be engaged in the larger world around them. They take up causes, whether it is the environment, LGBTQ rights, or gender equality.

In my conversations with groups of teens, I was pleasantly surprised to find how open and forthcoming they were on sexual preferences, same-sex relationships, and the acceptance of bisexual feelings amongst themselves. They were also much more politically active and outspoken about homosexual relationships, and they're bridging the gender gaps when it comes to discussions around what were earlier considered 'taboo' subjects, such as menstruation.

Tahira and her group of friends have tackled subjects like menstruation head on. 'In ninth grade we realized that we were more girls than boys, so first the dudes were uncomfortable with the discussions around periods, but they had to get used to it, they had no option, we're going to have periods for a long time.'

A turning point for them was the online survey they conducted whilst in the tenth grade with juniors in the eighth grade. They noted that the presence of eighth graders on social media was rising exponentially and they wanted to analyse their responses to questions on menstruation and sexuality, the LGBTQ community, and feminism. The 300 responses that came in were an eye opener. Whilst the data highlighted the progressive approach of the majority of students, there were also biases, prejudice, and a great deal of what they referred to as 'crazy misinformation'.

For instance, one question was—why do you think pads are sold in black plastic packets? And the extreme answer was—to stop the spread of AIDS, cancer, and arthritis. So clearly there was a problem of understanding, information, and perception. And what was their learning?

Tahira jumped in right away. 'The survey taught us a lot about totalitarianism. This constant need for the education system to appease parents is so wrong. When Section 377 was abolished, we went to our teacher and said we should do a school board on this to raise awareness, it's a great step. And she said no—parents will have a problem. We didn't know how to respond to that. It's like, yes, the entire world is being racist, but does that justify your being racist as well? If the school wants to teach students to be progressive, and think out of the box, you can't work like this, that's nonsense. And if you're going to appease everyone, how is it going to work? Is this how we are educating leaders of tomorrow? We weren't allowed to do the board, we fought and we're still fighting.'

There is a comfort and an acceptance about different sexual orientations though the schools are uncomfortable with such positions. Moyna explains further: 'We have a lesbian couple in our grade and they're open about it. The authorities haven't come down heavily upon them, as yet. Many boys look upon lesbian couples as sexual entertainment. And then there are those who aren't supportive of LGBTQ rights and they think it's disgusting. So they call things gay, which is not really homophobia, but I believe it's just discomfort. No male couples come out openly. Some say I'm okay with seeing girls kiss but I'm not okay with seeing guys kiss.'

Some are brave enough to be open and state that they are gay.

With sadness they remember a classmate who was always getting into trouble in school because he called it out. His parents sent him to a residential school, but there he was beaten for the person that he was. They abused him physically and emotionally for being too effeminate. Finally, he got admission to an international school overseas, and he's much happier there. 'He's a proud bisexual, he sensitized many in his grade to LGBTQ rights, and they were supportive. Our hearts went out to him because at such a young age he faced some vicious verbal bullying in school,' remembers Moyna, sadly.

Aman believes that acceptance of sexual preferences is definitely increasing amongst their age group. 'Thanks to pop culture, at least being homosexual does not make you an outcast as it did some years ago. It's a lot more open after the 377 judgment. That generated a lot of optimism amongst my peers—my Instagram was flooded with Yes Yes Yes Go Go Go…Gay Pride. I can't say the same for transgender rights.'

Kamini emphasizes the criticality of discussions around sexuality amongst the peer group and the need to develop empathy. 'It was when I went to college that I realized just how much homophobia there is in people. When 377 was repealed, there was a group of boys who we got into an argument with, who said that queer "Woh karte hai na, woh jo unnatural hota hai". They were junior to me and I couldn't believe the number of pages on social media that were full of hate for transgender folk and feminists—all run by women. I feel very privileged having been to a school where many people think like me, but at university many peers have faced rage and violence because of their sexual preferences.'

Exploring one's sexuality in the absence of reference points other than what appears on social media or the lack of a platform for discussion and understanding can create so much confusion and anxiety in young adults who don't see themselves as heteronormative or 'straight'. Our children's upbringing is gendered and that is further strengthened by schooling. With the internet, our teens are exposed to new ways of thinking, both progressive and prejudiced. As parents we are going to need to build that bridge of communication with our children, particularly when it comes to sexuality.

Kamini has an insightful observation. 'Parents shy away from talking to their kids about sexuality, because to some extent it means accepting the fact that your child is not a child. Actually, she is still a child but with a sexuality and those two things just don't come together sometimes in people's heads. They don't see that you can be sexually active and still be a child because you don't know what you're doing and are still as naive as any kid would be.'

Kamini was slowly coming to terms with the fact that she was not straight and didn't know how she was going to accept that. She shared her confusion when faced with the limited models she saw on social media. 'The kind of queer people that you see on Instagram, Facebook, and Twitter—they treat their sexuality as a very performative thing and it sets us apart. I didn't want to be a part of that narrative, that being queer meant being "different". Our phones bombard us all the time with images we want to emulate. You look at people and see definitions of being healthy, being feminine, being masculine—all these various ideals have been set for you and it's oppressive and we accept that to some degree.'

When teens have attempted to converse with their parents it has usually ended badly. Priya's experience was no different. 'There is a lot of discomfort when people 'come out'. I've seen people use the word gay as an insult and they are clearly homophobic. My mum asked me if I was a lesbian because I wanted to watch *Call Me By Your Name* and mum said she didn't want to watch two guys kissing on screen and I don't get that.'

Jyotsna attempted a conversation with her grandmother and parents about same-sex relationships and got a resounding no for an answer. 'She just said it's not natural. My parents might accept it from other children but me and my brother, no way. I was trying to explain to my parents what LGBTQ is and they started making fun of it and I was slowly getting angry.'

For seventeen-year-old Jayant, accepting different sexual orientations has come about only in the last few years, and it was triggered by the change in the law. When the son of a friend of the family 'came out', it led to a heated debate with his mother. 'I felt it was really impressive that he had the courage to do it and state it formally in society. But my mum felt it was a bit weird. In her opinion it goes against biology, it's unnatural, and against nature. So we argued. I felt people can love whoever they want, and I asked her what would you say if I told you I was gay? She looked at me long and hard and replied—"I'm sorry I'm not going to accept that". But then she went for the wedding of our friend's son and his partner and she came back impressed with their courage and bravery in taking their vows in front of their friends and family. I believe the whole attitude to the non-heteronormative stuff is a very generational thing.'

TIPS FROM OUR TEENS ON BRIDGING THE GENERATION GAP

Looking back to my own troubled relationship with my father, I wish I could have made him understand that I needed him to respect my right to individual freedom, to privacy, to choose my relationships, and understand what made me happy. His disapproval always came in the way. And, of course, we were never able to build those bridges or have the conversations that one does as a parent gets older, since he passed away when I was twenty-three years old.

I empathized with my students and their pushing back in their relationships with their parents. In my conversations, what came through was a universal need for conversations and communication that was non-judgmental. Gauri wryly observed that 'In my house, we don't talk about things that matter. It's all down to how you view your child. Parents don't view their children as individuals who have their own thoughts and values, who are not adults but are growing and developing and may have very real problems. If parents understand that, then there will be some mutual respect. If a child is coming to you and is distressed about a relationship, the response normally is to brush it away and say, it happens. Instead, respect your kids, understand that they are human beings with their own individual lives, and that may help foster better conversations.'

That word again. Conversations. It's a shrinking space in schools as well. And it is a critical space because everything cannot be taught at home, says Gauri. 'You can't sit children down and say—here listen—drugs—don't do—sex—no! Schools, too, need to identify the culture they want to have. They need to be open-minded and liberal. The school needs to understand that these are experiences the children go through and these need to be addressed so that the children are safe. And these conversations need to be open and non-judgmental. Sadly, the counsellor's usual solution to problems is, "Okay I'll call your parents!" But there is a reason that the child has come to you—schools need to have a space that is not judgmental, and teachers who are approachable.'

Vanita believes it is critical that we accept that we will all make mistakes—parents, children, and teachers. 'We forget our parents can make mistakes and it's alright to make mistakes, it's alright for your child to make mistakes. If your child at fifteen is going out and smoking a joint, it's part of the experimentation, but talk about it, step back, and look at what's important. She may have slipped up, but in the grand scheme of things, how does it matter, it's a blip. Because when it comes to talking about things that are actually serious then you're not giving them space to do so.'

Moyna remembers the conflicts she used to have. 'I almost left the house three times over common issues—like my phone and the laptop. My parents don't believe that you can only work with the laptop. They want to see me writing. And they don't want to see me with my phone all the time, which I completely agree with. Other than that, I accept that I have taken liberties, they have given me freedom which I have misused, and so they have grown suspicious about some of the things I do. If I lie, and by mistake, I'm caught, then I'm dead. But my relationship is evolving,' she adds, smiling.

Aman feels much more comfortable with his mum than his

dad, and the primary reason is the clash of value systems between his father and him. 'He has grown up in a society with a traditional mindset where you have to respect your elders. With my dad, when we talk, it's formal. It's sit down, talk, and make sure you don't piss him off by something you say, so it's strained. My mom is different, chilled out, so I have no problem in using expletives in front of her, talking about rap and rock music.'

Understand your child and their emotions and don't treat siblings alike is Jyotsna's advice to parents. 'My brother and I are polar opposites. He didn't care about anything, exams, courses, he was chilled out. I stress, am more hard working, and I like to prepare. He's social and not judgmental like me. If I have a problem with my parents the first person I go to is him. My parents are very critical to my face, and say nice things behind my back. Why? I would like to be praised for the effort and hard work I put in to my face. And then of course, my brother being an Indian male could do a lot of things that I still can't—he could go in Ubers alone, he could spend nights out with friends, that's off limits for me.'

As parents we underestimate the power we have to destroy our children's belief in themselves and their confidence, particularly in their early teens, says Kamini. 'Because it's an age where you are learning about yourself from what your parents say to you, about you. So if you hear trash things about yourself, you will feel like trash. So don't make your kids feel like they're trash. It's not disciplining them, it creates huge obstacles for them to jump over and sometimes they might not be able to jump over them.'

Hearing Kamini and Tarini share the relationship they had with their parents was warm and comforting. Kamini's parents connected with her on all matters and they set clear boundaries for her, but she was allowed to do a lot of things her friends were not. 'I could speak openly to my parents, we used to have open discussions, I could wear what I wanted to wear, I could have guys over, and this was not a problem at home. So, they said, "Okay you don't need to shave or wax your legs so we will not buy you razors, we will not pay for parlour visits", which seemed so oppressive to me at that time. It was very confusing because my friends' parents would insist on parlour visits, "You have to do this beta", and my parents were telling me, "No way in hell. You cannot get your eyebrows done, you have a mono brow, live with it". I learnt to live with the fact that people were not going to think less of you if you didn't wax!'

Tarini looks upon her parents as equals, they share the responsibilities of the house, so she didn't grow up with the stereotype that mothers look after the house and dads make the money. 'So, if I want to go somewhere I will not just ask my mum. When I was young, I used to confuse the two, I called my dad, mum many times and mum, dad. That is not the norm,' she says, laughing.

Clearly communication with her parents was easy and comfortable and according to her it's the way she has been raised. 'My parents are very open with me. Most of my friends have no clue about their family's financial situation. We discuss it openly. My parents shared the financial problems they were facing when we moved into our new house. They said, "Look we're short of money, so be careful". If you sensitize your children to touchy topics, they don't remain touchy. My friend asked her parents about their financial situation because of college and overseas costs, and they refused to answer. They said we'll figure it out, you have nothing to do with this, and that's not good for a number of reasons, it gets in the way of communication and trust and when she is an adult it will be hard for her to manage her stuff.'

What is the reason behind their supportive relationship? It seems to be untouched by the generational divide! According to Tarini, it's down to a combination of effort and communication. Although both parents work and don't get back till 9 p.m., they put in the effort to communicate. She shares her day with them, her feelings, even feelings she is ashamed to have—about her friends or her studies. 'And they do the same,' she says. 'My parents can be vulnerable with me. My dad isn't as easily vulnerable because he grew up in a very stern family where his dad told him, "You're a man", mum made him like that, she said "If you want to be with me, you have to be human". They're also like my best friends, and I know for a fact that regardless of where I am in the world and what I'm achieving, I'll still have my parents and that's really important.'

The psychotherapist Dr Gloria Burrett firmly believes in dialoguing between parents and children to make that critical connection. 'If you don't have a connection, no child is going to let you in. They have that one special button that says switch off and mute. And then the task becomes harder and you have power struggles. Do we as parents know how to dialogue? Can we learn how to dialogue? Do we know how much kids yearn to be dialogued with? I will never forget when a kid who came to me at sixteen, said "I wish my father knew I had a mind and that he could listen to that mind."'

Dialogue—it calls for both attentive listening without judgement and the freedom and security to speak your mind. To share your feelings without fear. It is the fear of being judged, belittled, and this fear shakes your sense of self and confidence. To be able to dialogue, and to make that effort to communicate and discuss uncomfortable matters is the greatest bridge in any relationship. At a personal level that has been my greatest challenge. Over the years I have realized that growing up in a home where conversations went only one way, where what my father decreed what would happen had me walking on eggshells all the time. My greatest fear was facing his anger and I saw my mother constantly anxious to please. I have always struggled with conflict, with having difficult conversations, and I would much rather ignore than confront issues, and I didn't realize this until my husband pointed out that I was passive aggressive. It has taken years of working on myself to stop being fearful of conflict and I truly believe that if as parents and educators, we can create these safe spaces for dialogue in our homes and our schools our children will not be bedevilled by fear and an erosion of their belief in themselves.

4

BRIDGE TO INCLUSION
THE DIVERSE NEEDS OF OUR
SPECIAL CHILDREN

We have no special needs children,
we only have just children…with special needs.

—Uwe Maurer

According to the World Bank, 1 billion people, or 15 per cent of the world's population experience some form of disability, and the prevalence of disability is higher for developing countries.[1]

In India, according to the 2011 Census, 2.21 per cent of the total population has a disability.[2] While taking into account the 2011 Census figures, the UNESCO 'State of the Education Report for India: Children with Disabilities 2019' states that three-fourths of the children with disabilities at the age of five years and one-fourth between five and nineteen years do not go to any educational institution. These are grim statistics and there is little understanding, support, or security for parents and children with special needs in our country. The parenting journeys of those who are raising and educating children with diverse needs are complex, emotional, swinging

---

[1]Disability Inclusion, World Bank, 14 April 2022.
[2]Persons with Disabilities (Divyangjan) in India—A Statistical Profile : 2021, Government of India, Ministry of Statistics and Programme Implementation, National Statistical Office, Social Statistics Division, www.mospi.gov.in.

between hope and despair, and critically, without the acceptance and understanding from our society and educational institutions.

There are a number of institutions in this space that have done purposeful work and it would be unfair to single out just a few. What has struck me about these champions for change, though, has been their passion, dedication, and resilience. Their vision for children has not only embraced schooling but also looked ahead to the challenges of young adults with special needs, the need for training, for jobs, and for assisted living and assimilation in society.

In the area of inclusion, there are two silent champions who are the pillars behind the improvements we have seen in both policy and implementation, and they are Meena Cariappa and Gita Dang. Their seminal book *Meeting Early Challenges*, first published by UBS in 2005, is a must read for parents and educators, particularly parents who are starting their journey with their special child. Their book needs to be translated into as many languages as possible and made freely available to the parents of the 12 million children living with disability in India.

The first step in this journey starts with the birth of your child and no matter what the level of disability is, nothing prepares you for what can only be described as a shock. There is the 'Agony of dashing from one place to another, not knowing whether they will find the answers to questions such as, what is wrong? Why? And most important, what can be done for my child?'[3]

Mohan is six years old and has cerebral palsy. CP is referred to as a bright mind locked in a body that doesn't function. His parents Seema and Ashok were kind enough to talk to me about their experiences, many of them harrowing, at the hands of exploitative medical practitioners.

Seema sailed through her pregnancy but during a troubled birth, the oxygen levels dropped and Mohan was born a preterm baby who

---

[3]Meena Cariappa and Gita Dang, *Meeting Early Challenges: Special Steps for a Special Child*, Noida: UBS Publishers, 2005, p. 3.

had two brain haemorrhages, and spent a month in the intensive care unit before he came home. They were told that their child might have some developmental delays, and an MRI after three months would confirm the nature of the developmental delays. She recounts with dismay that 'when Mohan was discharged, they presented us with a bill of six lakh rupees for the ICU. There was no counselling and no support. We knew that there would be problems, but we were not aware of what kinds of problems could occur and what our journey would be like. We had no idea how we would nurture a special child.'

It was only when they brought him home that they started identifying some abnormalities. 'Mohan was 1.5 kilograms when he came home and we noticed he was making himself into a C shape when he was lying on bed—his legs were not straight. We had to carry him around and take him out in the car, doing rounds of our colony, so that he would sleep. It was hard for the first few months.'

Three months later they went for the MRI, which was very painful for the baby. 'Post the MRI, the doctor told us Mohan had a problem in his cerebellum—and we still didn't understand what that was. We visited another consultant who confirmed it as cerebral palsy. That was hard enough, but we weren't aware of the challenges we would face,' says Seema, recounting the distress.

Then the vicious cycle of testing started. They were told by one doctor that he would need surgery to rectify the squints in his eyes. Luckily a second opinion advised eye exercises and the wearing of patches, so surgery was avoided. The next stop was getting his hearing tested—expensive tests followed and the hospital pronounced that he needed an expensive hearing aid because he had lost 99 per cent of his hearing. By now Seema and Ashok had realized they must always get a second opinion, and sure enough an ENT specialist confirmed that Mohan was absolutely fine and there was no hearing loss at all.

They began to explore options for therapies for children with cerebral palsy. 'So there was this NGO which administered hyperbaric oxygen which promised improvement. Again, it is so commercialized and they charged 1.5 lakh for two months. We were in our parental home in North Delhi, so we moved to South Delhi to be near the clinic. I never saw any improvement with the oxygen therapy. Other parents, whom I met at the clinic, privately shared with me that it was a waste of money. As parents of a special child, we are vulnerable and we see hope in every opportunity which may just be a money-making exercise,' said Seema.

The catalogue of charlatans continued. A homeopathic doctor in Pune claimed to have remedies for CP and after a few visits and expensive consultations, they discontinued the medication because Mohan appeared to be lethargic and listless after taking it. By this time, Seema had joined a group of 300 mothers of children with CP and she was told that the homeopathic medicine contained steroids—one of the parents had it tested.

There are so many instances of exploitation of vulnerable parents and gross malpractice where medical practitioners are endangering the health of children. It's criminal. The day I met Ashok and Seema, they had just returned from a session with a doctor who had written several books and claimed he had a successful practice both in the UK and Italy. He insisted Mohan had autism as well and that he needed to massage the coronary artery that leads to the brain. According to him, this would increase the blood flow to the brain and Mohan would improve. He charged ₹15,000 per session. Another friend of Seema's ended up paying ₹75,000 for five sessions in the hope that her child would get better. The parents now feel that they can tell a fraudster from a genuine practitioner.

What an agonizing way to learn this lesson, and how alone one feels. 'The presence of a disability in a child deals a blow of great magnitude to parents, and yet they have to come to terms with it and deal positively with it in order that life carries on for themselves and the rest of their family—the special child included. The feelings range from disbelief, resentment, guilt, blame, and finally—a desperate search for solutions.'[4]

---

[4]Cariappa and Dang, *Meeting Early Challenges*, p. 9.

When Rohan and Neelu were informed that their second born, a daughter, was a special child with Down's syndrome, they experienced the usual cycle of emotions—fear, anger, frustration, and disbelief. But they grew to accept the reality and decided that they would have a third child. Neelu shared their reasons for taking this crucial decision. 'Emotionally, I was feeling so insecure having had a challenged daughter, the whole purpose was for my own self-worth. The bigger reason was that it would help our son to have a sibling to take care of our daughter who was special. Coming from large families ourselves, we see the value of having siblings around us for support. I am very happy we took that decision, it really helped us having siblings around for Veena.'

And so the journey began, with the primary focus on speech therapy, ensuring that she was able to articulate her words and communicate with confidence. It was a strategy that paid dividends—early intervention with a speech therapist has ensured that Veena's social interaction is very good. She is a part of a large loving family, with lots of cousins around, so she is very comfortable communicating with those around her.

The next step of the journey is of course preschool and the difficult and painful experiences of finding an inclusive school that will admit your child. Seema and Ashok visited five schools where they were turned away because the schools said they were not equipped to handle a child with CP. 'Eventually we found Kiddies Corner, a small preschool nearby. They welcomed us and gave him admission. I believe we get blessings when we meet such people. They were also open to keeping him on in school for another year in case he did not manage to get admission into a regular school. The fees were nominal and they made Mohan participate in everything,' says Seema. And Veena, too, was very fortunate, the legendary Cherry ma'am at Shishu Van was progressive and compassionate and a fervent believer in inclusion, and Veena joined a school where she was happy and loved.

Other parents are not so lucky and many hopeful parents are

just turned away at the gate by the security guards. They don't even make it to the reception to present their application. There are, of course, exceptions, and St. Mary's School in Delhi has led the way with Principal Annie Koshy, who has always opened her heart and doors to parents and children with special needs. And as she recounts—it all began with Sam.

SAM'S STORY IN ANNIE'S WORDS

'Sam was the brother of a student, and they lived across the road from the school. The mother came and told us that Sam, who was in the eighth grade at the Spastics Society, was getting very bored at home and requested us to admit him to our school. So we said, "Okay, let him come". In spite of all our ignorance. Sam did well, he went on to do his graduation from St. Stephens in Mathematics and was the first student at St. Stephens in a wheelchair and now lives independently. Mrs Anita Shourie of the Spastics Society personally came to talk to all the children about Sam before he joined. She spoke to them and said, "Look, Sam is embarrassed about being dependent on all of you, and he feels he is really troubling you. So he will not ask, please put on the fan, or ask him if we wants some water, it is better you should ask him."'

'We learnt that it was about our change rather than getting him to change. We didn't have a lift or ramp or anything but we would always say—"so who are the strong boys in the class?" And they would rush forward and pick up the wheelchair and go up the stairs with Sam. He could not move at all, and he had to piddle into a bottle, but the boys got into it wholeheartedly.'

'We understood so many things through Sam. We understood the stress on the parent when we noticed that Sam's shirt would be soiled when he came to school every morning. His Dad told us that after he was bathed, shaved and fed, he would vomit, and he would have no option but to take him to school with a stained shirt.

'We got a writer for Sam. We realized that since his speech was so poor, he would be unintelligible to a scribe, so his tutor was allowed to write for him. We also made a breakthrough with the CBSE to allow children with special needs to use computers. We even went to court against the CBSE to offer children alternative questions in geometry. It was all because somebody was in school requiring something that needed to be pushed.

'This kind of resilience is also building up in our teachers. You have to address the needs of the children.'

As Annie talked, I wanted to burst into applause. 'The counselling department has instructions that when you receive an application for admission from a child with special needs, whether we have seats or not, we will meet the parents. So that someone is able to vent, and we try and give them advice on where they could go. If the parent himself needs training for a child with autism, then Action for Autism offers that. Emotional resilience is critical not just for children but for parents.'

Annie couldn't have said it better. 'At a basic level, all children are different and you can't put a square peg in a round hole, you have to change the hole, and we were making those adjustments for our special children. A child needs to go to the second floor—come on, let us carry him. If he's going to the toilet and he's a crawler, we have to make sure that the toilet is dry at all times. When you have children with special needs, your methodologies change, and they become more child friendly. And that little boy in the corner of the class who is not presenting any issues, but is quiet and by himself, actually benefits, because he sees the changes you are making for this little one out here. I believe inclusion has played a very big role in the mental health of our institution.'

'We need to practice empathy and sensitivity all the time. I tell my team—don't lose sight of the goal. We get caught up in the faff around schools and we lose sight of the children who are at the core of what we do.' And that sadly is a principle that schools overlook most of the time.

When it came to admitting Mohan into a regular school,

Seema and Ashok were fortunate to get the support of a friend and meet with an empathetic principal. 'The principal was warm and understanding but sadly that did not percolate to the deputy head and the teachers,' says Seema. 'I slipped into depression and had to go to a counsellor for therapy because my experience with staff down the line was so hurtful. I felt tortured. I had to accompany him, and sit separately with him in a room, while the rest of the students were engaged by the teacher. They did not allow a shadow teacher and didi to be with him. I was there the whole day and had to carry him everywhere. I had a bag, bottle, Mohan, my stuff, and they would not let my husband enter the class.'

Talking to parents with differently-abled children who came for the admission of their child, I can remember in many cases, how silent and distressed mothers usually were. The fathers would do most of the talking, in a few cases mothers crying silently, eyes downcast, holding the child. So many mothers, when alone, said they felt they were to blame. The in-laws could, at times, be hurtful and cruel and sadly many couples drifted apart, sometimes the mother preferring a divorce to the daily round of shaming and instead choosing the responsibility of raising her child as a single parent.

SCHOOLS AND INCLUSION

Now, thanks to the intervention of the Delhi government, it is mandatory for private schools to reserve 3 per cent of their seats for children with special needs. This is a part of the 25 per cent reserved for underprivileged children. Anurag Kundu, chairperson of the Delhi Commission for the Protection of Child Rights, believes that Delhi is perhaps the only state where this significant step towards inclusion has been taken. It comes with several challenges.

However, in 2018–19, the *Hindustan Times* reported that there wasn't enough of an uptake. Only 53 students got admission against the 1,322 seats reserved for disabled children in entry-level classes of nursery, kindergarten, and class one. A section of parents seeking enrolment of their children said that the schools they have been allotted are not equipped to cater to the special needs of their children.[5]

Seema and Ashok accept that it's a helpful and useful step. Mohan's school is supportive, but at the end of the day, the parents feel that the school does not want to take responsibility for a special child. Keep in mind that Mohan has a shadow teacher and a didi accompanying him to school, paid for by the parents. The feeling is that the special child is the responsibility of this supporting team and not of the class teacher or the assistant teacher. The faculty lack an understanding of what the disability is, and how they need to be cared for and how they can learn.

'Teachers should be encouraged to handle children of different disabilities. They don't understand what CP means. All the special children are put in the same bucket—autism, CP, Down's syndrome, slow learners. To them they are all the same,' says Seema, sadly.

Anurag shared his learnings from school visits to St. Mary's three years ago and the important lessons he learnt from Annie Koshy. 'We were going to conduct school evaluations and our framework had questions on whether the school had special educators, held special classes etc. She corrected me—the job of the special educator is not to teach. That results in segregation within a school. The job of a special educator is to hold remedial classes, for sure, because they need specialized techniques. The primary job of a special educator is to enable all stakeholders within the school, including other teachers, to be able to teach a child with special needs. The remedial classes bridge the problem. The primary job of teaching that child lies with the mainstream teacher, not the special educator. That way you take responsibility. Right now you believe that a child with special needs is the responsibility of the special educator. I too hadn't thought about this, it's only when she said it I understood I have to take a position on this. This is a cultural problem. Every teacher should

[5]Fareeha Ifthikar, 'Private schools admitted only 53 disabled kids in entry-level classes', *Hindustan Times*, 13 February 2019.

learn to engage with a differently-abled child.'

Unfortunately, as I write, the critical components of understanding disability and equipping our teachers at the pre-service training stage do not exist. There is no comprehensive module in the pre-service training programmes for teachers who graduate with a bachelors in elementary education or any other degrees. As educators, our expectations of the achievements of the special child need to be realistic and not just focused on academic achievement. A small step for the special child could be a major step in her development progression.

Neelu and Rohan experienced this with Veena when she went to a Delhi school where the approach to education was traditional. 'She kept getting zeroes in her academics and they expected her to develop like all the other children. They didn't equip them for a practical life. There was a separate section for children with challenges but the focus was on rote learning and academics, which was unhelpful. We wanted her to develop living skills, which would allow her to live in this world in a practical way,' says Neelu.

For Seema and Ashok, report card days were particularly difficult. The teacher could not understand that in a special child, the improvement curve would be very different. The class teacher always felt the pressure to show improvement, and would insist on 'improvement'. They always felt a lack of acceptance and this was especially evident when the children performed at assemblies. 'Mohan was segregated to perform separately so that it would not affect the performance of the other children. I had to intervene and say that I would hold Mohan and stand with the other children, and that I would make sure that the assembly would go ahead smoothly. So yes, the teachers need to be sensitized,' adds Seema.

Entry into schools does not mark the end of the journey—it is only the beginning—for the future of both parents and children is uncertain. There is the critical phase of adolescence—guiding them through the confusion of mood swings, growing sexual awareness, and the vulnerability of special children is a matter of great concern.

It is so important for parents to address the issues around early puberty, and help children understand that their bodies are changing and cautioning them about being touched inappropriately. Neelu and Rohan understood the need to set boundaries for Veena, just as you would for any teenager. Neelu has talked to her at length about a good touch and a bad touch and periodically would ask her if she was uncomfortable about anything. 'I have had a lot of chats with her. Even today, unfortunately, she is still searching for a boyfriend and she is still hopeful that one day she will marry. It's a natural need, her mind and body have developed and I can sense the need she feels to be like her peers. Luckily, she gets distracted because of her huge social circle of friends and she has a job, but periodically she does talk about—"Why can't I also get married?" And that's a difficult question, and while we keep finding ways to convince her that she will find a partner, I know that she won't be deluded for long,' admits Neelu.

But in many cases, parents have resisted these conversations and Carol Paul, a special educator and consultant, recounts the recent backlash from parents at an inclusive school where they held a meeting for parents around these concerns.

'It was almost as if they were living in a different time zone. They were attacking the counsellor for answering the questions their kids had raised, and refused to believe that children had asked such questions. One child in class five had asked the question, "If I want to have sex with my own gender, is it all right?" Parents need to understand that children are sexually aware. They have been exposed to so much in their homes, stuff has been shared and they haven't been given a context.'

'The parents didn't want body parts to be named! "Why have you talked about a penis as a penis?" There was a child who said that they don't like their cousin coming to visit because he keeps pulling the child's nose. And the parents have been telling him, "That's because he likes you and he is affectionate". But actually what was happening was that the cousin had told him that his penis was another nose, so his penis was given the name of a nose. And the parent doesn't know because the parent hasn't taught the child the other name. Clearly, there was sexual abuse going on, and the parents were refusing to accept it,' says Carol distressed.

Children with special needs are particularly vulnerable to sexual abuse. Carol explains that 'If they've experienced it, they would want it, because they don't attach any emotion to it, it's a physiological requirement and they would do it. And we do know young women within the groups I have worked with who have been abused by their driver, by their help at home, or indeed family and friends. Parents have come to know about it and have not removed the home help/ friend from their environment because that person will go out and talk about it.'

Unless young adults understand social media friendships—whose invitations they should accept, how much should they share, the doublespeak of online communication—we cannot be sure that children are safe online. Children are vulnerable, and they must know that real-life friendships should be a pre-requisite to communicating online.

She gave the example of fourteen-year-old Amyra, who made her driver a friend on Facebook. He began to write all kinds of things to her on Messenger. He told her he would use a different name. So rule number one for parents—do not create social media accounts for your children who are underage by fudging their ages. Using social media and online platforms has become a very important part of the lives of children with different abilities. There are a range of benefits, from becoming more independent, to finding their space with others, and discovering new interests. Parents and carers need to take some important steps to safeguard them from risks. Other than monitoring them closely, setting boundaries and limits on the time they spend on platforms, they need to ensure that their children are using privacy settings. It is also useful to form family and friends social groups where you can guide them collectively and limit the risks they would face with strangers.

Carol explains, 'You have to be able to be a part of the

conversation that your kids are having online and be able to bring to light what is okay and what is not. They need to learn how to read social media behaviour and that is difficult for many. They send various kinds of emojis without understanding what they are truly expressing.' The language on the internet is intentionally obscure and full of doublespeak.

She cited another example of a young woman with special needs who is a successful hacker on Facebook. So she creates an account in the name of someone she knows, let's say in the name of Abha Adams, and invites others onto that page. People think—oh Mrs Adams has invited me, and they become friends, and will have entire conversations with her thinking they are talking to Abha Adams. She told Carol she had been doing this for several years and admitted that when she became obsessive about somebody she became a stalker. So there's no parental monitoring there. Typical children also have these problems when they are younger, and it's the same with special needs kids.

Shalloo Sharma counsels parents on building relationships with their children, being vigilant and careful at all times. They must ensure that that they know their children's passwords and check that they are not sharing personal information on social media platforms. After all, as Shalloo says, 'It is a platform for validation, every "like" is a visual validation and you have to make sure that they're getting their validation elsewhere otherwise they will keep seeking that on social media. You have to let them go through that process of counting their likes, feeling elated when they have enough, or distressed when they don't. They won't be able to bypass it, but as parents we can help them through it.'

Shalloo and her team went on to develop a module on dating for differently-abled teens and they had a tough time convincing parents about that. 'How do you teach a young man that if he likes a girl, this is how he is should talk to her? How close can he stand? They need to understand the subtle art of flirting. We also have a module on a simulated coffee shop where you are trained on how to ask a girl out for coffee, questions like, "Can I sit with you? Can I buy you a coffee?" Why are we not teaching them these skills?'

For parents, perhaps the hardest subject to tackle is the one on sexuality. Shalloo works with parents to overcome their hesitation in talking to their children about gender and sexuality. Typical youngsters have their friends to talk to, they can go to websites, read books, share experiences, and build up what they know. This group of youngsters with special needs will first turn to parents, and if they don't get the correct information, or if parents put a lid on things, where are they going to go?

Shalloo is direct with the parents. '"Just because he can't read and write with the ability of an eighteen-year-old, you may think he doesn't have sexual needs. Please don't forget that their bodies are growing up and there are going to be very normal and natural sexual urges." Unfortunately, when I use the word masturbation—I can see them visibly take a step back.'

In her experience, parents of girls find it much harder to have conversations around sexuality because they are constantly anxious about their safety. 'They are not thinking of whether she may have needs and that she may want to be with a man. But does she have the skills to express herself? Does she have the strength to take the emotional rejection that almost inevitably comes?' asks Shalloo. In a society which is repressed about addressing sexual matters or indeed acknowledging it as a normal and natural part of human life, most parents are embarrassed about any conversation around it.

Parents are also rightly concerned about their children's presence on social media, which makes them particularly vulnerable. Yet, if done correctly, the digital space can be a haven for young adults with diverse needs. Youngsters who have trouble making friends right away can meet people who are like them—there is no judgement and they can talk to people online and that's really good for them. Loneliness is always a few steps behind the special teen. Rohan and Neelu realized that as the other children in the family were growing up and moving away, Veena was beginning to get lonelier. Acknowledging the need for her to have a social circle, they brought together a group of girls and along with other parents, they have consciously worked hard at providing them the opportunities to connect over experiences, as well as creating experiences for them.

'A lot of our anxiety is diminished because they're on the WhatsApp group, and they are on it all the time. They squabble and make up, but they support each other. I wish I had so many friends. They can spend nights at each other's houses, we can travel as parents without worrying what will happen to our girls. Before we pack, Veena is packed to go and stay at Karuna's house. The emotional support they share works as a safety valve, and whenever any individual anxiety arises, they manage to diffuse it between themselves,' says Neelu with a smile.

So cyber space can inform and support in many ways. Carol Paul gives the example of Prateeksha Gupta, the founder and CEO of an online speech therapy and communications organization. 'So a parent sitting here can get speech therapy for their child without having to run around. Kids can connect emotionally and not feel alone. Even some of our kids, who want to talk to us, can get on to a Google Hangout or a group meeting on Zoom and they look forward to that virtual gathering, and for an hour and a half we have this chatter and it's like a social hub, but in cyberspace.'

So for all the reservations about digital spaces, they can be harnessed for our young teens. Children need this connection and validation of friendship. Especially when you consider the challenges they face—starting with the need for social acceptance, the struggle with academic pressure from a system that doesn't adjust itself to their needs, and the bullying that leaves them hurt and bewildered. They yearn for friendships and face rejection when they are 'blocked' by their peers on social media, and all the while they are witness to their parents' growing stress about their presence in the digital and real world. Their helplines are parents and siblings, and Shalloo believes that parents who stay vigilant need to ensure their young adults receive the necessary training, communication skills, and security of being able to have honest conversations with their families at all times.

INCLUSION IN THE WORK SPACE

I have always loved this quotation from authors Liz Fosslien and Mollie West Duffy: 'Diversity is having a seat at the table, inclusion is having a voice, and belonging is having that voice be heard.'[6] Whilst it was quoted in the context of organizational work cultures, it resonates strongly when we look at the challenges faced by young adults with diverse needs in the work space.

It is in the work space that, as a society, we need to work so much harder at inclusion. According to a report in the *Indian Express*, out of the 1.3 crore people with disabilities who are employable, only 34 lakh have jobs. UnearthInsight, a marketing intelligence firm, believes that with the right policies and strategic shifts, employment opportunities for people with disabilities can be enhanced.[7]

That's what Shalloo Sharma set out to do when she started Evoluer, which means 'to evolve'. She wanted to focus on inclusion, in society, in jobs, in social circles, in malls, at parties, and in marriages. In her words, you cannot be inclusive in school and then stop it there. She realized that once young adults with different abilities finish school, they really don't know where to go and what to do. Suddenly, for this whole group of young boys and girls, who felt so much a part of the school community, their template of life is broken. Social differences widen. They ask—why can't we go to college, where have my classmates gone? They are without an academic structure and without a social group, and parents were finding it very hard to come to terms with the lack of opportunities for their children. Where do they go now?

So Evoluer takes students who will benefit from being in the

[6]Liz Fosslien, Liz and Mollie West Duffy, *No Hard Feelings: Emotions at Work and How They Help Us Succeed*, London: Penguin Books Limited, 2019.
[7]PTI, 'Half of the disabled population in India employable: Report', *The Indian Express*, 15 July 2021.

same ability group, and Shalloo consciously facilitates things they could do after the skills program is over. Understandably, there is a considerable amount of engagement with parents. 'There is counselling, helping them organize group activities, and encouraging them to stop treating the children like babies. We organize outings, have a separate group for girls and boys sometimes, girls go for pedicures, boys go for a soccer matches—I don't want to sound gender biased! But the attempt is to make sure everybody is in touch with everybody else.'

'Side by side, we teach them skills that maximize their social interactions. And then of course there are the outbound camping trips and travel that they love. They need these experiences to have something to talk to with cousins, they need as much exposure to experiences as possible. We know that as young people the most fun times we had were when we were with friends. And if that's not happening then that's a big gap. We have to provide the scaffolding for the longest time. But I strongly believe that they will get to a point where you can step back.'

Other modules include work skills, social skills, and life skills, including the digital space, traveling, and bits and pieces of independent living. A large part is computer technology, and of course communication and how they can use the internet for stuff other than watching YouTube videos. They make videos, they post them online, and are taught the power of accessibility through technology.

And all of this is an interface with the work space. This focused approach to mainstreaming is quite novel and Evoluer has succeeded in getting them jobs in a mainstream environment. They focus on the skills of the future. So far skilling had been limited to pre-vocational, vocational, handicrafts, basket weaving, and pickle making. Shalloo quite rightly sees computer skills as neccesary for the future.

'It has to be an industry that will have enough work for everybody. Retail, e-commerce, hospitality—these are the sectors that I'm looking at and these are the skills we really need to focus on. Everybody has their laptops, they have their journals and time tables on their laptops, they need to know data entry, know Excel, to make presentations, and be able to talk about current topics,' she adds.

The great news is that Evoluer has been able to place at least 50 per cent of all the students in internships and jobs. But there is another very successful dimension—and that is the personal one according to Shalloo.

'When you look at a classroom of young men and women, they are talking and laughing about things that their age group should be—about bunking class. They know that they can crack a joke and everyone will laugh in the right context. When you see an undercurrent of the female/male group dynamics happening, that's what I call a real success. When they're on their own WhatsApp groups, when they're hanging out after college, when they come up to me and ask—When can they have another outing? Can they just stay on a little longer? When we were shut for Covid-19, everyone was texting—Can we come anyway? We're doing Zoom classes, which is fantastic. When you look at a Zoom class you see how brilliant things can be when they have the skills that are needed.'

Some of the students have gone back to college, having picked up the skills to navigate courses. And a few others have gone on to start their own entrepreneurships. A lot of youngsters with special needs get into entrepreneurship in the digital space, through social media or online businesses. For example, Sachin has autism and he makes chocolates. With the help of his parents, he launched Sachin's Delights, a homemade chocolate business, which became a hit with many, all thanks to Sachin's marketing on social media.

What appears to be heartening is that the industry has been forthcoming and if a firm has not been able to take on Shalloo's students, they have been directed elsewhere. Making corporate spaces more disability-friendly and inclusive is also exhausting for Shalloo as she waits for the Amazons and Dells to wake up and understand the worth of this batch of very computer-articulate people.

Societies marginalize communities by making them 'invisible'. Just as women were behind doors, behind veils, or walking behind their menfolk, in some societies we tend not to see the aged and the infirm that are hidden away. But in our society, sadly, we have drawn a veil over disability as well. People with disabilities have no presence in schools, colleges, shopping centres, parks, and even in social gatherings in our homes.

Whilst talking to senior students in an inclusive school on the subject of diversity, I asked the class how many of them were aware of the range of disabilities that many of us lived with, and if they had known or met young teens with different abilities socially, in family gatherings or amongst friends. For a moment there was an unfamiliar hushed silence in a normally animated class. Then very slowly, hands began to go up, and encouraged by those who went first, other hands raised themselves. That forty-minute class has been one of the most meaningful moments in my career as an educator. Students shared, perhaps for the first time, their concerns around their ignorance and awkwardness at being around those who had a disability. A few spoke about siblings with challenges who were not acknowledged by the larger family, about how the family rarely spoke about the needs of their special child with the other children. It's almost as if there is a silence around acceptance and acknowledgment, very much like the silence around mental health.

Shalloo Sharma weighed in on this, pointing out that while we have gender studies in our school curriculum, we don't have diversity studies. All the parents I spoke to make a strong push for the need for inclusion in all spheres of life, else how will we ever know what each individual's true potential is? You need one person with diverse needs in a large organization for that whole organization's perception to shift.

It is imperative that we view the bridge to inclusion as critical and we need more and more schools to embrace inclusive practices. When children of all abilities learn and grow together, there is an understanding, an acknowledgement, and a warm acceptance of diversity. Shalloo explains this with passion, 'If someone has not met, seen, or experienced a person with diverse needs, haven't seen them working, functioning, smiling, and being, they will not "know" them. We need to push visibility.'

I don't think people are deliberately being obtuse. It's just that they don't know. And there are prevailing stereotypes which we are all guilty of. We used to say, "Andha ho gaya hai? Behra ho gaaya hai?—Are you blind? Are your deaf? I have known people whose needs are different and that's why I wouldn't use those words nor allow anyone close to me to do so,' says Shalloo.

As parents of a special child with CP, Seema and Ashok have experienced this lack of sensitivity first-hand. 'When I take Mohan to the park in his pram, people stare at me as if we are criminals. They need to understand that it is God who has given us a special child. I face it each and every minute. When I go to my in-laws' house, we have to park our car and walk 600 metres, and I fear that walk because of the way people look at me and my child. Even at school, when I took Mohan for assembly, when we walked off the stage, all the parents stared at me, looking uncomfortable, as if my child and I had no business to be there. Inclusion is so important, and for Mohan, who has no friends, his world is his family. But when children grow together in an inclusive school, acceptance grows within the group and I am so happy that over time the children in his class have accepted him.'

Social acceptance and recognition from institutions leads to acceptance from the family and community—and not just in terms of reservation and quotas. Support groups are a source of great strength for parents of children with diverse needs. They provide solutions, an opportunity to learn from each other, share advice, and group members who are always there to listen to each other. We need a proliferation of these support groups to help parents draw upon others for the strength and advice they need on their journey. Drawing strength from each other, parent support groups create communities that step in to help each other, provide forums for sharing and discussion, and welcome volunteers to spend time with the children while they attend meetings. In Chennai, VOICE (Voice of Parents for Inclusion, Care and Empowerment of Children with Special Needs, was started with ten parents, and has grown to nearly 2,000. Similarly, SCAN (Special Child Assistance Network), which has over 3,000 members on its Facebook page, organized live calls and activities during the pandemic to help parents keep children engaged and share their own challenges and difficulties.

I requested all the parents and specialists I interviewed to share their learnings and advice with other parents. What follows is a moving collection of what they had to say:

'Parenting a special child is for life. It is a situation that stays with you and there is no shortcut and you can't run away from it. It's important that as parents we don't see it as a "problem" and stay positive. There needs to be an acceptance of this reality. Special children are the way they are, your child is not "diseased", and you cannot focus on looking for a "cure". When this acceptance is missing, unscrupulous doctors take advantage of it and prey upon the hopes of the parents. So stop thinking of "correcting" the problem', says Neelu.

'Every special parent needs a guide to tell them how to think about their situation. Someone to help you change the mindset with which you approach your child's disability. The journey is very different, it's very long, I remember the guidance I received from my biggest support—she said everybody has a problem. Some problems are unseen and some are seen...it's challenging but it's life. Positivity is the only thing that will support you. I think all parents of special children should share their experiences so that people can learn from each other's mistakes and successes,' says Seema.

'The most important thing is acceptance. Yet, train yourself to let go. It's tough. But if you train yourself to let go, you'll be teaching them the skills that they need to move away. You need to step back. The sooner you start treating them like adults the easier it's going to be,' says Ashok.

'As parents we need the support of other parents like us. My husband and I have learned to take time out for each other as a couple. You need to be doing stuff in your own lives that fulfils you as well, because if you put all your energy and hopes on your child, it's going to be very tough,' reiterates Neelu.

'By making your special child a part of your life experience and helping her create her own life experiences, scripting her own narrative—she will learn to own it in due course. Don't overpamper and don't overprotect, it does sound difficult, and it is,' says Rohan.

And in unison they agreed—no silence around diversity. There should be no isolation. The mantra has to be integration.

5

THE SILENCE AROUND THE MENTAL HEALTH OF OUR CHILDREN

The silence around the mental health of our children has always worried me. Ask any educator and they will agree that the last ten years have seen an escalation of issues and concerns around the mental health and emotional well-being of our children. And we have good reason to worry. Globally, in the last fifteen years, researchers have given us increasingly alarming statistics on the sharp and steady increase in childhood mental illness that is now reaching historic proportions, and the pandemic has escalated that even further.

Approximately 15 per cent of children and adolescents globally indicate the prevalence of mental health disorders. It is recognized that 50 per cent of mental health disorders begin by the age of fourteen and 75 per cent by the age of twenty-four, and this makes child and adolescent mental health a global priority.[1]

Closer home, the statistics are even more worrying. India is the most depressed country in the world, according to the World Health Organization, followed by China and the USA.[2] Even as suicides are completely individualized in society to absolve our state institutions of any responsibility, suicide rates in India are higher than the global average, highlighting a burgeoning public and mental health crisis.[3]

---

[1] L Bruha, V Spyridou, G Forth, and D Ougrin, 'Global child and adolescent mental health: challenges and advances'. London: J Prim Care (Abingdon), 16 July 2018, p. 108–9.
[2] 'India is the most depressed country in the world', *India Today*, 10 October 2018.
[3] 'Story in numbers: India has suicide rate higher than the global average' *Business*

According to the National Crime Records Bureau's Accidental Death and Suicides report, student suicides spiked to 12,256 deaths in 2019–20—8.2 per cent of the total number.[4]

We are also seeing an increase in learning disabilities, communication, and behavioural disorders[5]—more and more students are being diagnosed on the autism spectrum and with attention deficit disorders—and in this context, we realize the significance of inclusive education. And perhaps the most worrying of all, the rates of depression, anxiety, and self-harm in our young have increased. In essence, India is facing a serious mental health crisis, with an estimated fifty-six million people suffering from depression and thirty-eight million from anxiety disorders, according to a report by the World Health Organization.[6]

The National Education Policy (NEP 2020) has proposed to make the counselling of parents mandatory so that students have a stress-free environment at home. The data indicates that mental stress is one of the most common factors behind student suicide. What is happening and what are we doing wrong? I spoke to established therapists working with children and parents to understand the scale of the problem.

A CHANGED LANDSCAPE

Family therapists and child psychologists Dr Shelja Sen and Dr Amit Sen found that the landscape had changed dramatically on their return to India in 2003 after an absence of eight years. 'When we came back we found that services for children's mental health were few and far between. We realized that in the larger scheme of things,

Standard, 13 October 2019.
[4]Serish Nanisetti, 'Student suicides go up', *The Hindu*, 27 November 2021.
[5]Nayana Mariya Kuriyan and Justine James, 'Prevalence of Learning Disability in India: A Need for Mental Health Awareness Programme', *NIMHANS Bangalore*, April 2018.
[6]Dalbir Singh, 'Combating the mental health crisis in India', *Indian Express*, 7 February 2022.

the understanding of mental health was very low and child mental health was an even lower priority because it doesn't give the revenue and the quick buck that other services would,' Dr Shelja told me.

This is echoed by psychotherapist Gloria Burrett, who returned from the UK in 2006 and set up her practice at the Shri Ram School and Sitaram Bhartia Hospital. She was shocked by the fact that children and adults were coming out of the woodwork seeking help. 'We were having to push people out of the door, even during our lunch hour. At school, it was kids dying to talk. It ranged from adoption issues to family breakups, custody battles, and parents' mental health issues leading to anxiety in kids as young as class one.'

Dr Shelja paints a vivid picture of the ground reality that faced them. 'There has been a huge escalation (in mental health awareness) in the last ten years. The number of children we are seeing has escalated like how! And we're getting younger and younger people with mental health difficulties—cutting in young children as young as nine- to ten-year-olds—depression, anxiety, suicidal thoughts and intent, OCD, eating disorders, and bipolar disorders. And along with that we have the neuro developmental difficulties like ADHD, autism spectrum, and learning disabilities.' Parents and children are struggling with family and relationship issues, but Dr Shelja cautions against using the term 'epidemic' to describe the situation because it implies it is an illness that is spreading, as if it is a cultural trend or a transmissible disease.

To my interminable question of why this is happening, her response was both wise and measured. She believes that we have to look at the problem from the larger lens of the society we live in. 'It is society that's broken and not the children. Children are the canaries of the time, they reflect what society is doing and feeling. As a society we are going through a huge amount of disconnection... while being connected 24/7 on our phones and social media. But in terms of meaningful connection—we are losing out.'

I asked Dr Shelja what she meant by 'meaningful connection', and as she explained, it's all about acceptance—accepting who we are and not having to pretend to be anything else. 'That connection is one on one, here and now. But if my connection with you is on social media all the time, on the number of likes and the number of followers, and if my worthiness comes from that, then we don't spend time in conversation with our loved ones.'

Her words mirror the thoughts of the teens I have spoken to. How the whole issue of reputation, popularity, and image starts at a very early age, with beautiful girls believing that they are fat and ugly. Children are afraid to share personal struggles with friends in case it ends up on social media. Petty fights go up on social media, and when that happens you cannot have conflict resolution, because the pain is too deep. The pressure is on students and parents to be what they are not. Of course digitization feeds into this because, as Dr Shelja explains, 'When I'm feeling disconnected I look for that connection more and more in the virtual world, on social media, and I try to portray a certain image, a certain look, because that's what's giving me the validation. It's a false world I am building up. We find parents coming to us with concerns about the children's internet use or addiction, and we look for a reason for that. Why is the child addicted to that? What is happening? And many times we find that the child is struggling with depression, and the depression could be due to academic struggles. She has never had a sense of doing well and there is a sense of being shamed.'

At times their only escape is the high they get from the gaming world. The dopamine rush from this experience is much more fun than the real world. 'So we have these young kids who have completely stopped going to school. They are sitting at home, up the whole night on *Fortnite* or *Counter Strike* or all these games, because that's where they're getting that sense of connection, it's a pseudo connection, but it is a connection. In the real world they have no connection, because there they have to prove themselves to be somebody, and they can't because they think they are failures,' adds Dr Shelja.

We touched upon the KGOYF (Kids Getting Older Younger

Faster) phenomenon and the problem Gloria notes is that they're growing up faster without any accompanying resources. It's a time when they need mentoring adults more than ever.

'So I can get on to the internet and onto a porn site in class five and no one is telling me about it, no one is making me aware about what might happen, what are the pitfalls, I don't know what's going to help me. The more opportunities I have of growing up faster, the more I need the mentor, the wise other, the wise elder in my life.'

And the absence of guidance and mentoring results in confusion, anxiety, and panic attacks as early as classes five and six. There is also the possibility, says Gloria, of a very quiet depression which results in possible self-harming, but the seeds are sown very early on. So what is at the heart of that depression? 'There's a sense of hopelessness and futility settling in very early, and so much of it is linked with, "If I can't perform in class, I can't compete with the others, I don't have a sense of my own strengths and well-being, coming back to I am not good enough". Finally, they get to the point of feeling "I'm going to be left behind, what's life worth?" And that's when they need that mentor to steer them through this.'

Gloria has started a pilot project—a group for adolescents where they can share their feelings and thoughts in a safe space. 'When we met for the first time, everyone in that room felt as if they were alone and no one else was struggling like them. They shared that they seek support in the virtual world, visit self-harming sites—such is their desperation for help. Fifty per cent or more in a class are self-harming, in my experience. Some have called it a collective symptom while others dismiss it as attention seeking. But why would I need to go to those lengths to seek attention? It's when all the other stuff has not worked—so I have to up the ante to say something is confused and struggling inside me.' Some of the first questions she asks is if any of them have had suicidal thoughts and how many are self-harming.

Gloria has led a series of master classes on parenting challenges. Her advice to parents and teachers is always kind and useful, and it has certainly made me think more deeply about my own parenting struggles. Relationships between parents and children need a balance—particularly when it comes to power—and she uses an interesting code to explain this.

'The green is where you have the power and the red is where I have the power. If we don't have that balance then I'm going to seem over-powerful and imposing on you and you're going to hit back to prove you are also powerful and are the boss. If I win every battle, you will feel resentful and then power struggles and revenge will play out. And the only way children can take revenge is by saying no… exactly when they know it's going to hurt. Think, are you holding too much of the red; are you saying no too often?'

'One mother said to me, "I don't understand the problem, I just say no to this and this and this." My response was, "You just said you tell your child how to eat, how to dress, when to get up, you nag him about x, y, etc."—we had twenty instances. So record your conversations with him tomorrow and see what it picks up about your communication and, sure enough, it went all her way,' Gloria said.

Dr Shelja also believes we don't give our children enough space. 'Children are being told all the time what they have to do. They have no sense of meaning about what they are doing and why? It sounds existential, but there is a lack of agency about their lives.' She makes a crucial point about the need for nature and the outdoors in the lives of our children. 'Take the child who is addicted, shut down the internet, take away the gaming devices, he will shout and cry, but let him loose outdoors, and he will be completely different.'

Above all else, what distresses Dr Shelja is our surrender to the digital world and our complete lack of understanding about the manner in which companies have put billions of dollars into research and algorithms that can exploit our children. 'We think when we get on to social media we are consumers. We are not. We are just products. Our children are just products for them. They are using our kids, designing these games in such a way so as to get the child hooked. It's highly addictive and there's a certain normalization of this addiction which is so damaging.'

Surely, parents are thinking clearly and deeply about this? Dr Shelja believes that when faced with the addictive nature of these products, parents feel powerless and helpless. 'So what do they do— they restrain the children, take their phones, but after some time, under pressure, they return the gadgets.

Dr Shelja believes that the shutdown cannot happen by individual parents, and it has to happen at a larger level. She believes, 'To have more conversations with children, helping them understand how these companies are exploiting them. Children have a strong sense of justice about things and once they understand the exploitation, they'll get it, and they'll have a sense of agency about the choices they make.'

She believes that the scale of the problem is such that 'If you ask any family if they have been touched by mental health illness, you will find that every family has someone who is affected; you ask a class, every child raises their hand, they all know someone who is struggling with mental health. Parents too exhibit high levels of anxiety, they struggle with a sense of worth, a sense of self, and then find it difficult to give that calm, steady support to their child. It's a feeling that I'm not good enough, so my child has to make sure that he is good enough to make me feel good enough.'

This fear and anxiety about whether their children will be left behind in the race for college admissions, jobs, and successful lives forces parents to focus on the child's academic achievements at the cost of their mental health. When parents come for counselling and they are confronted with the fact that their child has anxiety/depression or other mental health concerns, their responses are distressing. 'Okay, but will this affect his grades? The child sitting with them wants to kill himself, he is suicidal, but despite their concern their focus is on—'Boards mein kaise kareyga? Admission mil jayega ke nahin?'—How will their board exams go? Will they secure admission in a good college?—she tells me, sadly.

It appears that our social structure has brought into existence the assembly line of school, college, and job to be successful, which fuels the anxiety in parents, children, and society at large. As a narrative therapist, Dr Shelja uses the mantra—'The person is not the problem. The problem is the problem and the problem is social. Children are just reflecting what is happening in our society and so are families.'

So how do we start addressing a problem which is social, cyclical, and which would involve engaging with all the stakeholders—students, parents, and of course teachers? The solutions lie only when we work with them as a community. And the point of intersection where all three come together is the school.

It was this realization that made Rajani Khanduja decide to move to a school nine years ago after having spent several years as a mental health clinician at a hospital. At St. Mary's School, she got the opportunity to work with a community and, as she pointed out, 'Here, I am not waiting for problems to present themselves, here I have a finger on the pulse.'

The professionals I met and spoke to agreed that pre-emptive work was the key to addressing the problems we are seeing in schools, both amongst parents and children. And let's not forget the burden of responsibility now appears to be focusing on the teacher in the class. As educators, how many of us are equipped to help, support, and deal with mental health concerns? Our training certainly doesn't cover this at all. Therefore it is imperative that we start with the training of the teacher in the classroom.

Gloria's advice to teachers is to constantly look at the personal lives of the students and understand what is happening in their homes. A teacher's understanding, observation, and investment could help with an early intervention. 'I found that when a child was not sitting in class, when a child was not completing the work, when the child disturbed the class, then we were called in. But the quiet kid, the kid who had something happening at home, the kid who doesn't have friends, those are the kids that go under the radar. And a lot of our preventive work with the teachers was "This is the child you need to refer to us, look out for that one."'

The strategy of creative writing and picture composition reveals a lot about how the child is feeling and is indicative of problems. Gloria recounts an instance when, 'The mother came to me and said, "I am leaving my husband, don't tell the teacher, I don't want her to look at my child differently". But it was obvious in the child's creative writing! In this nursery class they were given this picture of a forest and had to write five lines about going into the forest, and this child wrote, "The baby's going into the forest to find his mummy and daddy". So the psychological projection is significant.'

The onus on schools, educators, and counsellors calls for an integrated approach to mental health that signals, 'It's okay to talk about it!' At St. Mary's they have developed a vision for emotional well-being and the department of counsellors headed by Rajani is supervised by Gloria once a week. They are clear that you need to work with the whole community and it is centred on pre-empting problems.

The school has circle time practice where they go for group counselling into the classes, talk to the whole community on appropriate issues, and prepare them for the stages of their development. They also work on areas of sexuality and relationships, study skills, bullying, and all matters related to growing up, including the changes in their bodies when they hit puberty.

It's a challenging task but for Rajani it's also extremely fulfilling. 'In our school we have students coming from children's homes and child care institutes so we know that they have a history of trauma. This may manifest itself in the form of aggression, some are silent pleasers, and we know how important it is to work on emotional nurturance. You work with the community. You work before the problem happens. I find this very uplifting.'

Taking children from children's homes is a conscious policy decision St. Mary's has taken, and this act of courage and empathy, according to Gloria, sets them apart. 'The amount of mental health issues that this school contends with is mind boggling. They take children from children's homes where you have kids who've been traumatized. They have fathers in prison, so there is no parent here for them to have a support structure for the child. It's staggering. But at St. Mary's they always say, "Come, we are here for you". They act almost as surrogate parents. They enter the battlefield knowing what it's going to be.'

Courage and openness in a school system is the key. It's important to send a message that it's okay to talk about it rather than hush it up and hope it will go away as so many institutions and parents appear to be doing.

For instance, at St. Mary's they don't shy away from talking about sensitive subjects such as abuse and explain POSCO to the children in student assemblies. Students are aware that 1098 is the ChildLine helpline and understand the support they will receive. This gives them the confidence to speak about what is troubling them and they don't feel the need to brush things under the carpet. Rajani gave an example of a graduating student of class twelve who told her, 'I don't know how many are coming to you, but you have changed my script!' He used to come for counselling and his classmates would make fun at him, saying, 'Arrey, yeh to counsellor ke pass jaata hai'—he goes to the counsellor.' He had a bad condition related to Obsessive Compulsive Disorder (OCD), and he said he wanted to talk to others about it in an assembly and share his experiences with the whole school, assure others in his condition that it was treatable and why they must seek help from the counsellor. Now there's a validation of good practice when students take it upon themselves to spread awareness and sensitization, and are unafraid to stand up and be counted.

Acceptance of each other is at the heart of an individual's well-being and getting children to accept each other, as well as converse, is a strategy that Gloria has used very successfully. She created social skills clubs at the Shri Ram Junior School and handpicked the children—those who desperately needed friends, those who had a lot of friends; kids blessed with wonderful social skills, and kids who were a motley crew, so they would learn from each other. 'It was so amazing that every child there benefited. So everybody in that group had some issues, and every term we changed the groups and we did one session a week. What we tried to establish in these groups was to really get to know each other. Put different kids together, mixed genders, children with autism in there, with ADHD, just get to know each other as people and look at the commonality that we all share,' she says with a smile.

Interestingly, the strategy uses the technique of 'hot seating', a convention used regularly in theatre practice. Each child takes a turn sitting in the hot seat, and the others learn how to ask them questions out of curiosity, questions that may help them know the other, rather than challenge them. For Gloria, a revealing moment came from students in class five.

'We had this very dark kid who was in the hot seat and the first question from a little girl was: why do you cry in school? And the little boy says: because I'm bullied. That was her question and having asked it, she ran to the back to sit down. Next question was: but why do you cry every day? His response was: because I'm bullied every day. So that questioner went to the back of the line. The third one was: what do they bully you about? They call me 'Kallu' he said, and I hate it and I cry because none of you stand up for me. And the fourth question came from the girl who is very socially skilled. She sat there, and said: what do you want us to do? And he said: whenever you see it, just say, knock it off! That day when I went into the lunch room, he's across the room and he looks at me, gives me a thumbs up and says, "Ma'am it worked!"'

It's moments like this that make you realize that teaching is a vocation like no other! It's critical for an institution to have a finger on the pulse and create safe spaces for discussion around issues that arise, issues that children are discussing and are confused about. Take Article 377 for instance. When that was repealed, while one school refused to allow students to hold a seminar or allow the ninth graders to create a student board around it, the Shri Ram School took another route. It was the first school to invite chef and restauranteur Ritu Dalmia to talk to parents, students, and teachers from across all the three campuses about sexual preferences. The discussions were open and humorous, it went viral and sceptical teachers were taken aback.

As a counsellor, Shania's message to kids who are not heteronormative is—'"Hey I see you, I respect what I see. I don't judge what I see." We need to understand that we are a huge part of the support system for a child. The child needs to know that it's okay to be who I am. But if as schools we fail to give that space, we have failed them.'

Gloria reiterates the need for acceptance and how every child needs to know that a different sexual orientation is normal. 'There was a sixteen-year-old struggling with his sexual orientation, and he said: 'If only I had another sixteen-year-old who was going through it, who could tell me it's normal, who could regularize it for me. As students...we do not have safe spaces within which to talk. When we connect, what do we do? We're smoking up, or getting drunk, or we're talking about sex. No one's talking about your vulnerability and my vulnerability. So we don't have spaces for adolescents to talk to each other.'

Good practices towards our children's well-being cannot rest with just the school, a critical third dimension is the partnership with parents. Several years ago, while addressing a parent school association, a parent spoke of the relationship between school and home as a three-way handshake! I have never forgotten it, it sums up the interdependence between the major support systems that should exist for every child. It was so very different from the reality of my own school days. I cannot remember a time when my father went to my school, let alone remember which class I was studying in. My mother on the other hand, being an educationist herself, assiduously attended to the collection of reports every term—but there was no lengthy detailed discussion or interface with the school. Mental health didn't present itself as an issue. Little did we know then, that all was set to change.

The teachers at St. Mary's realized that they needed to bring the parents in. Parent workshops are held very regularly, on the third Saturday of every month. Rajani asks them critical questions around what they perceive are the concerns and questions their children are talking about at home, and how these could be jointly addressed by both the school and home. To her surprise, parents mostly respond by saying that they depend on the school for these answers, because their children are not open with them. Clearly the space for communication and connection was being overtaken by the busyness of parents' lives.

She notes, 'There is so much going on in the lives of our children. Earlier, family members used to be present for nurturance but that's not the case now. We see the spurts in aggression and depression in our children, and they are always linked to something happening at home. Sometimes there is domestic violence, or they were divorcing, or perhaps last night the parents fought. So whenever there was a behaviour manifestation in the school and we talked to the parents to take care, we come to know, "Haan abhi to jhagda huwa tha, iski pithai hui thi, mama alag ho rahin hain, papa shaadi kar rahe hain"—we fought recently, or we hit the child, or his mother has been living separately, or the father is getting married again.

Rajani finds that the root of the problems that the children come to her with lies within the family. It stems from something happening at home which the child is not able to process, not able to make sense of, and this in turn reflects in their behaviour at school. 'I sometimes wonder whom to work with! There were three instances last year where the father had died and the mothers didn't tell the child that your father is no more. The child was clearly showing symptoms of distress. She was disruptive, hyperactive, because somewhere the child was aware of what had happened. But the mother had not acknowledged this, had not grieved or mourned with the child. It's then that we end up working with the parent.'

Significantly, they began to focus on father–child relationships. Every Saturday, the fathers would come with children and they participate in workshops conducted by a sports organization. Kids had fun and bonds were formed. After enjoying the outdoors many fathers and children went on to have breakfast together. Rajani thinks back with a smile, '"Children said, Papa late aatey hain, par ab wo aakar kuch kuch masti kartey hain, khelte hain"—Papa comes late, but at least he comes back and plays with me and we have a good time. We did this because we saw that fathers tended to be absent from their children's lives. It's important to see the patterns that are emerging and then doing certain things around them.'

Annie Koshy, principal at St. Mary's, believes there is a crisis of confidence in parenting because parents themselves are so caught up in their worlds and 'This crisis is exacerbated because people don't pause to think things through. We are in constant dialogue with parents, pointing out to them where the fissures and cracks are in their lives.'

Many schools have parent-teacher associations and in many cases it is a perfunctory group that falls in line with the school. And yet there are several instances where the PTA can be the start of forging a community in the truest sense of the term.

At St. Mary's, the parent-teacher forum is also very strong. 'We make sure that we get those who are talkative and unafraid to speak their minds. We keep telling them that the children don't need their money, they need their time,' says Annie.

She received their support at a critical time recently when the school suspended a group of thirteen-year-olds who had called a fellow student and harassed her by asking her inappropriate questions about what she was wearing and made gross suggestions. This happened as soon as the school break started and the girl was very disturbed when her mother brought it to the school's attention.

'So over the holidays we held an enquiry, spoke to everybody, and they were suspended for three days. When school reopened, two parents who had not been in town descended on us, and the parent-teacher forum was meeting that day in the library; I was downstairs. They met me and said, "Ma'am how can you suspend our children." Their point was that their child did not say it so why should he be punished. My argument was that this was a collective effort of a group of boys, and while one may have done the talking, all those who were there were complicit because the speaker phone was on. They were very upset, and frankly, so was I. I went to the parent-teacher forum and presented the situation to them, and the forum called them down! I had told them that I was liable to go to the police because it was a cybercrime under POCSO. It was the parent-teacher forum that decided that I should call for a meeting of the POSCO committee and conduct an enquiry. So the committee met and felt that a complaint needed to be lodged, so now it has been lodged as a complaint with the police and has gone to the juvenile justice process.'

Pulling parents into decision making and discussing the issues around the lives of our children is critical. 'I always tell the parents, if you have a problem with a decision that the school has taken, come and speak to me in person, do not discuss it in front of the child. When you bad mouth the school and teachers in front of your child, they will not have any respect for the school. Kids get the message, "I can take the BMW and kill somebody but my father will stand up for me, he will lie for me". Parents need to know the lines and the expectations. Like any school, we have issues, but we address and resolve our issues. We are a small school, family run, so I guess we manage and we don't have the pressure of the return on investments that others have to deal with', says Annie.

Unfortunately though, most institutions are much more comfortable with burying contentious issues that involve the law, for they are in constant fear of the school appearing in the press and losing its credibility.

More and more schools find themselves in the role of instructing parents on how to parent in the complex times that we live in. Manika Sharma, the director of the Shri Ram Schools, bemoans the fact that parenting has been outsourced to schools. 'In the early 1990s, we had no counsellors, and no special educators. But we, as teachers, equipped ourselves to address their needs. I sometimes wonder whether with the addition of the experts we have become so dependent that we absolve ourselves of our total responsibilities.' In a sense, this was echoed by Shania, who spoke of how, from a collective society, we have moved to an individualistic approach and we have lost these connections. 'Parents have stopped being parents, they take the role of a child and they're finding it hard to navigate.'

This disconnect between parents and children is growing and becoming more pronounced in schools across geographies and demographics. A class teacher with over twelve years of experience, Janani says, 'I hear the same thing, in elite private schools, in international schools, and even with an NGO like Disha, where a teacher has come from a small town near Bikaner—he's also talking about the same thing. There is no connect between children and parents.'

And the disconnect plays itself out particularly for our teens as they battle with issues of their sexuality. Shania shares the case of one young teenager who is gay and struggling with owning her sexuality. 'There was a lot of pressure from home. The parents would come to the parent-teacher meeting and say, "Please ensure that my daughter is not hanging out with a certain student". And there was a constant threat at home—"I'm going to tell the school principal that you're a lesbian". It just broke my heart. So when the school announces we're organizing a talk on sexuality and sexual rights, it sends a strong message across, that we're here with you, we're standing with you and supporting you.'

Given that children are sexually active now as young as fourteen, schools that run sex-education programs have adjusted them by including appropriate information and ensured that the parents are a part of this dialogue with the students. Shania explains that before conducting the workshops for the children, discuss with parents the areas they will cover. 'When the counsellors, the school system, and the child are speaking the same language, it's very empowering. Unfortunately, over the past few years the number of parents attending these sessions has been dwindling, and that is a problem.'

Parenting workshops are gradually becoming an important part of the school's functioning and spaces for discussions with parents are being created outside of school. The Indian Express group has held a number of such workshops led by Gloria, which have been very successful. Judging by the responses of parents, Gloria notes that parents are 'Very well intentioned, but they themselves have never experienced finely balanced parenting which involves listening, letting the kid feel important, sharing power, and realizing when you can give in and when you pull back.'

The questions parents raise range from—'So if my son is getting up late, could it be adolescence? Is it normal, a part of his age development? When should I freak out, when should I not freak out? Is my freaking out making it worse and severing the relationship?'

She believes fervently in conversing with children and in making that critical connection. 'If you don't have a connection, no child is going to let you in. They have that one special button that says, "switch off and mute". And then the task becomes harder and you have power struggles. So can we as parents learn how to dialogue?'

I loved the experiences she develops for the parents. She asks parents to get their children to write them a letter, put it in a sealed envelope, and bring it to the workshop. 'Get your child to tell you something about themselves that they want you to know which they think you don't know—what do you think has been their greatest achievement in the last year? What do they love about you being a parent? What is the one thing they really want you to work on? Bring that letter in, sealed. And at a particular moment, we ask them to open the envelope. And then we all learn to listen.'

What followed were a series of personal revelations. After the session one mother came to Gloria in tears and said, 'Look what my thirteen-year-old daughter has written. "Mum, I've been trying to tell you I have been self-harming, but you don't get it. You don't listen. I've been trying to tell you take me to a therapist, you say it's okay, these are growing pains, we'll handle it." That mother said, "You've saved my daughter's life."'

A father stood up and read his fourteen-year-old daughter's letter.

'Dear Papa I hope this letter doesn't disturb you…. I hope you're not angry with me…. I hope you're not angry with me.' He said he never realized his daughter was struggling so hard to please him and not get in his way.

For Gloria the question was, 'Do we know how to talk? Do we know how much kids yearn to be acknowledged? I will never forget when a kid who came to me, at sixteen, and said "I wish my father knew I had a mind and that he could listen to that mind."'

I thought back to the interminable clashes with my father during my years in college, his inability to accept my rich friendships with men and women, my theatrical escapades, my love for trekking in the mountains with them instead of going on family holidays with relatives. We never spoke to each other. He raged. He never raised his hand—he knew that I would leave home as I had frequently threatened to do. My mother would get caught in the crossfire, and my dear Nanaji would drink an extra whiskey on such evenings, muttering that his son-in-law lived in the Stone Age. But never did we speak to each other and know the other's mind.

Gloria explains that as we feel more and more insecure and inadequate as a parent and a teacher, our go-to place is controlling behaviour, which is where we feel strong. The core of the workshops has been to get each adult individual to work on themselves and get in touch with their own authentic selves. We will need to shed our own baggage and be more self-aware. In her words, 'It's the wounds we carry forward that enter our parenting and that enter our teaching.'

Her advice to parents is wise and encourages them to reflect on their goals as parents. We want our children to be happy, but we define that happiness in our own terms, ergo, academic success, financial success, security, and status. She flips it around and recommends that as parents we should aim to make our child feel comfortable in their own skin, resonating with their own passions and interests. 'As a child I begin to feel good about who I am, I don't have to adapt to my parents expectations and I don't have to please in order to be liked!' We cannot only continue to support our children if they meet our expectations.

Gloria gives her own example of unconditional love and regard. She approaches every child this way—'When I tune in to a child, I say, "You are worthy of my love just by being who you are". I don't have to say you are worthy because you got 80 per cent. Forget about the performance, look at the effort and affirm that effort. The child then stands a chance to be a child with a growth mindset ready, to try again. Rather than to say, "I failed, no point in trying again."'

She believes, the lesson for parents and teachers is that every child is worthy of respect and it is our responsibility as adults to get them to experience respect for who they are. Respect will determine the way we set boundaries, discipline, and play out the consequences of their mistakes. She questions with feeling, 'Why do boundaries have to come with strictness and rudeness and humiliation and why do we rub their noses in it? What if I just say "I'm sorry, child, a deal's a deal, you've got to stay back". Why do I have to make them cringe and feel bad? At the core there should be respect for every human being. If that really pervades us, then it is a good start.'

Her closing words are profound. A child's sense of self comes from the expression on their parents faces when they look at them. 'That's the mirror they use to frame how good or bad they are. So tone it down, look for what's good. These are simple things. So what gets in the way? Maybe the parents' lifestyle, their wounding, their frustration, maybe a bad marriage. So to treat the child, the first thing is to look at the adult, the parent.' So start from a place of love and openness, be present and listen and that will lead to emotional well-being in your relationship with your child.

WORKING WITH TEACHERS

In this three-way handshake, the role the teacher plays is critical, since she is almost always the first point of contact for the child, the first to sense something is wrong, the first to begin to address it, and many times it takes resources and skills that she does not have. Teachers play the role of counsellors for parents and children, we depend on them to have the solutions, but institutions don't spend enough time considering that the teacher has to be happy and well in her own life, to be able to take on the challenges of her wards and their families. The balance we seek from parents, the listening, and the respect that we have spoken about, relates to the teacher as well.

Gloria questions whether schools are ready and willing to invest in the mental health and care of both parents and teachers. 'You get teachers who are grumbling all the time. Where is their support system? If the management can't hold staff, then the staff can't hold the child. Everybody needs to be held.'

She believes that social empathy, inclusion, equality have to be a part of every educator's DNA. 'And the first step is to get your teachers really sensitized. Choose your managers well so that they are constantly modelling respectful behaviour. Kids love teachers who are strict. There's one teacher who tells her students, "You're an effing idiot," and they love her because it's not said with disrespect and she'll give credit where it's due.'

Given our experiences of trauma and stress through the pandemic and its impact on students' and teachers' well-being, there is an urgent need to go beyond the traditional approach to teacher training. As educators we will need to develop attentive listening skills, be cognizant of students' concerns and demonstrate understanding as well as empathy. Continuing to check in how students are doing, engaging children in making the classroom a welcoming, safe, and comfortable space, being attentive to changes in children's behaviours, and modelling good coping behaviours for students—being calm, honest, and caring.

In addition to the above, valuable strategies are suggested by educator Marie Amaro who says we should be teaching students about strong emotions, encouraging the use of gratitude journals, giving students positive time-outs by incorporating a calming space in the classroom available for them to use, providing opportunities for students to air their opinions and problem-solve issues in the classroom, and building agency by giving them a choice in what, when, and how they work.[7]

As a practitioner, Janani draws her inspiration from the book *Tao of Teaching* by Greta Nagel. She puts a question to the teachers, '"How did you become a teacher? Is it out of compulsion, choice or chance?" If it's out of choice, they have really embraced the training. If it's out of compulsion, they've struggled to see sense in it and think it's too much effort. And if it's chance, there could be some wavering intent around it. But what is important is to open a window around it and show them the possibilities.'

Changing the narratives of children, helping them find meaning in their lives requires a great deal of investment on a teacher's part, Janani points out. 'You have to give up on a lot of your free time sitting in the staffroom. You have to be ready to be in the class before the kids come in so you can see them in the unstructured time. What are they talking about? What's going on in the classroom? How are you going to deconstruct it to make meaningful for them?—that requires time and it's a personal commitment and many teachers really make that effort to do it.'

Creating safe spaces for students, teachers, and parents to have conversations around both personal and social issues that affect their lives cropped up time and time again in discussions with educators. Finding the time to have these conversations in schools, which are usually over-scheduled, is problematic. Equally, parents find it hard to find time within their busy schedules and asking an already burdened educator to give up her precious time with her family can be a huge ask.

Manika Sharma believes that school managements need to work at freeing up teachers a bit more. 'A teacher has papers to set, board papers to correct, profiles to write—you need to free her up for at

---

[7]Marie Amaro, 'How to Improve Student and Teacher Wellbeing at the Same Time', *The Highly Effective Teacher*, accessed on 1 August 2022.

least an hour and a half a day so that she can invest in her class. We can keep offering all the training and workshops but when will she plough all of that back?'

In a novel initiative, TSRS has developed a structured mechanism for teachers to stay connected with students beyond academics. Mentoring modules for students are created on a monthly basis by the counsellors and these are scheduled into the timetable. Shania explains that, 'Mentoring modules are mental health capsules that we send to teachers across the school from classes six to twelve. The teachers deliver these in a Circle Time format which goes all the way to class twelve. In a month you'll have two mentoring modules. Every Friday, for one hour, you get to connect with the larger student body, and it's sacrosanct.'

Interestingly, the mentoring team involves the psychology teacher, the games teacher, the librarian, and those members of staff are picked who are close to students. 'They get feedback from kids about what is concerning and troubling them, and these are then knitted into the themes of the mentoring modules—we do work around compassion, sensitivity, and integrity.' With senior classes, mentors address the thorny issue of public displays of affection (PDA), consent, and safety. 'The kids keep questioning the school's problem with PDA. If we don't talk about this, who will,' says Shania, laughing.

At the heart of it all, though, is the trust that the student needs to feel when they come to their teacher and talk about anything that's worrying them. One student sought Shania out to talk to her about his sexual performance. A difficult subject to broach, but he did it because he knew he would not be shamed in the process. She believes it is critical that teachers understand that 'If we normalize shame or violence, we perpetuate the idea that it is okay to be in a relationship where you are shamed or subject to violence—it is not your fault. And how we talk to our children about these things is so important. Even a tone of disgust or a tone of, "I don't approve of this", results in an immediate disconnection. I tell this to parents all the time. Let's say your fourteen-year-old is struggling with his sexuality, I tell parents, "You don't have to say this immediately. It's okay to say to your child, okay I need some time, let me equip myself with some knowledge and let's talk about this again." It's okay to show your vulnerable self to your child.'

As a psychotherapist, she believes it's a privilege to work with kids. 'When people ask me, what's your job? I say I am a curator of narratives. I work with people on their healing journeys. I don't heal them, I work with them. They go on healing themselves and I'm a partner in that journey. Also, in a school, you're not just a counsellor, you're so much more, and you have to be able to deliver that,' ends Shania, quietly.

CLASSROOM COMMUNITIES THROUGH THE POWER OF
CIRCLE TIME

The therapists and educators I spoke to were emphatic and convinced about the power of Circle Time when it came to alleviating emotional distress and building resilience and empathy within the school community. What is Circle Time? How does it work? Can anyone do it? Do teachers need to be trained to be effective?

Dr Shelja Sen's favourite teacher is Janani Iyer and her second book, *Imagine*, is rooted in what she has learned from her. 'She is one person who created that space for parents, and for each and every child. I have learned the power of creating classroom communities from her.' Janani is a beloved and successful educator who has fine-tuned the art of Circle Time and developed the acronym CAN—Cohesive Communities, Affirmations, and N'riching Narratives.

I meet Janani a few times and I'm struck by her warm, gentle, and empathetic presence. She is working consistently with teachers to help students to counter the anxiety that's eating up our young teens. She believes that the depression, self-harm, and self-loathing that has set in them is due to the chokehold of social media on today's teens and the subsequent loss of real communities. 'They're finding communities on Snapchat, Facebook, Instagram and that can only be countered by creating supportive classroom communities. Its heart wrenching to see the burnout that kids reach by the time they reach class six.'

As a teacher in a classroom the question she asks herself is, 'How can I create a safe space for my children?' She proceeds to deconstruct a safe space and Circle Time for me and clearly there is a systematic process but more importantly it's a culture that needs to be built. 'So every time we sit down to have a conversation, there has to be a round of creating a safe space for that conversation. So we do a round of, "If I have to speak without inhibition today in the group, what do I want from all of you?"'

'It's a safe space that is defined by the children. So someone will say, "Today I need listening, nobody looking at me, or making faces, or I don't want anybody to talk about what I have spoken." Somebody will say, "I need trust today", another will chip in with, "I need a little laughter". So we know that it will keep evolving. At the end of every Circle Time we need to celebrate how much of the safe space were we able to create! It has to be an ongoing process. But every time we sit down, there has to be that ten minutes of creating that safe space. It cannot be compromised' and Janani asserts that over time, the regular Circle Time becomes a culture.

I can see that as a result of this what gets created is a feeling of community! Each and every child feels that they belong—'I don't just fit in, I belong.' Janani believes that creating classroom communities has been her most important commitment in the last ten years. She realized early on that parents had to be brought into this community. So she turned the typical parent-teacher meetings on its head and the orientation at the start of the year focused less on information (which was sent earlier) and more on conversation!

'I remember when I did it the first time, I was very scared when I introduced the idea of how it takes a village to raise a child. I put that on the board and we had exercises around it. I explained that your child will grow only when the whole community grows.' So she asked them: 'What do you expect from the school, what do you expect from the children, and how can we contribute to this goal of becoming a community?'

A counsellor carried out a similar session with their children in another room simultaneously, and in the last fifteen minutes the children came in with their goals for the year ahead and shared it with their parents. And the parents shared their goals for the year and there was a conversation amongst the adults and the children jointly sculpting the year ahead through conversation, communication, and connection.

So, let's take a look at some of the goals of this particular classroom, co-created by students and parents along with the class teacher. These were created after understanding the individual needs of the class eight children and the group needs as a whole. The endeavour was to achieve these through open discussions, stories, teamwork, circle time, drama, and other activities throughout the year.

1. A sense of belonging to the group, building trust and acceptance, creating opportunities to work in groups.
2. Better relationships between the children and the adults and more engagement.
3. Appreciating self and others, identifying one's own strengths, respecting individual differences.
4. Asserting oneself in conflict situations but keeping an open mind during disagreements and learning to be patient in conflicting situations.
5. Sharing feelings without inhibition, giving meaningful feedback, and taking feedback.
6. Dealing with anger and articulating one's feelings and empowering children to identify and resolve their inner and interpersonal conflicts.
7. Creating space to make mistakes.
8. Building a sense of perseverance to complete tasks and manage time and resources.
9. Handling disappointment and failures and building resilience after setbacks.

10. Learning to work in a team and making choices with responsibility—understanding freedom comes with responsibility
11. Taking responsibility for one's actions and understanding consequences
12. Openness to new experiences, understanding social media etiquette, and developing respect for the dignity of labour.
13. Creating opportunities for individual and group conversations.
14. Developing a need for inner quietness through mindfulness.

It is an exhaustive and impressive list of goals, but does it work? Does it change class dynamics? How do the children feel? Every class that works with Janani on the goals writes a report at the end of the year, and here are some snippets in the voices of the children.

Our class is a diverse collection of bright, fun minds, each unique in their ideologies and executions. Our goal has been to make sure that everyone feels like they belong, because each student contributes a vital ingredient to the intricate recipe that is 8E. Through our various mentoring sessions and class discussions, we set out to achieve a balanced, complementary class.

This year we learnt to make our own decisions. We learnt people are not always what they seem and that everyone is going through something in life hence we should reserve our judgement.

We put emphasis on thinking out of the box and aspiring to make a change through initiatives like the period box, various conversations, and openly discussing social evils and problems plaguing society like the Sabarimala Temple case.

Our class has really worked on giving everyone the ability to disagree. Various 'arguments' have not been resolved, yet everyone was given their own space and not attacked for voicing an unpopular opinion.

It has been a miraculous year as we laughed together,

cried together, and worked hard together.

Families fight...a lot. And that's what our class is. We're a family because families don't only fight but they are also able to come out of the fight smiling and closer than ever. We stick with each other, help each other do better and our class would be incomplete if even one out of the thirty-two people in our class were absent.

Can we really bring about such reflection and cohesion in a class through this process? This might appear to be a flash in the pan, but Janani shared a few other reports, one from class six and another from class seven and I would have loved to print them in full but here are some excerpts, again in the children's own voices.

Class six students call themselves the Dynamic Dynamites. Their greatest achievement they felt was to develop a more inclusive attitude in class and making an effort to include the new children who had joined them that year. The group worked on listening to each other, respecting every idea, and respecting secrets.

They elected their class representatives in fair and open elections, created budgets, raised money through their own efforts to create a class stationery budget! Boys sold sweat bands, key chains, football posters, and even joined the bake sale—they collected ₹3,000.

Finally a recent report from 7A batch of 2020 as they think back on their journey.

The year began with groupism and no unity. We were busy in our own little world. We bore grudges, were disinterested, completely disorganized and most boys and girls did not talk to each other.

Our teachers were frustrated because we did not submit our homework on time and our academic performance was not up to the mark. Janani ma'am was disappointed with us because we were laid-back and we never honoured our commitments, we did not appreciate each other and were self-obsessed and self-centred and not inclusive.

We decided our goal was to make the class a better place. We celebrated birthdays every month, every morning we appreciated two–three of our classmates and we introduced the buddy system. So five buddies were in charge of five students and helped them organize their work.

We had a Circle Time which laid out expectations. Messages were sent to parents with the homework details, books were lent, and many of us showed immense improvement and we cleared the backlog of assignments!

So what was the result of our hard work? We are now trusting, united, helpful, supportive, respectful and organized. Most teachers now love working with our class and we have had fun!—dancing, award ceremonies, class assemblies, hilarious circle times, serious circle times, and we leave with phenomenal memories!

Janani puts it down to the power of communities. 'If the community gets established, I have been amazed at the way in which they hold each other. There are classes where kids are dealing with a divorce at home and the community is standing by. I have seen it work every year for the last ten years, but you have to invest in it, and you have to give it time, you cannot speed up the process.'

Janani ensures that she draws the parents in to support class initiatives. A few years ago she noticed that the children from the economically weaker sections were struggling to keep pace with their academics. She brought class parents in for a conversation and they decided to create an academic support system for them. It was the community deciding to help, and they did, one parent and their child even made audio notes for the children who might not be reading as swiftly as the others. Such is the power of community and kindness.

Janani has some unconventional strategies—throwing the teacher's table out while meeting parents and sitting in a circle. She is also mindful that every parent comes with their own personal narrative, with aspirations and failures, and she has learnt to respect that. The result is the creation of safe spaces and strong relationships in her classrooms.

She is quick to point out that there can be pushback at times. 'It depends whether the school has a progressive philosophy and is empowered to act according to it. When I trained a school group recently on Circle Time, I asked them to consider that when they deliver it to senior students, there will be topics that come up for discussion that the faculty have to be prepared for, like masturbation for instance. Immediately, there was a pushback. There was no way they would allow that because they considered it a perversion. I was saddened by that, because while they were courageous enough to introduce Circle Time, they were not courageous enough to give the power to students.'

'Students will want to ask about menstruation, sexual activity, contraception, and the boundaries around all these issues. These are conversations that kids want from their teachers. If, as a teacher, you are unable to handle this conversation and say so frankly, the kids would respect you. But if your position was that you believed these things should not be spoken about, they would not spare you,' Janani says with a smile.

Gloria, too, realized that unless teachers experience mentorship at a personal level they would not be able to become and give mentorship themselves. 'So we started a sensitivity group as teachers. If they experience what it's like in a circle, it will then flow through them to the kids. So we tried different things to get kids in an ethos where the adult says, "I am here for you, I will put my books away to listen, to say, tell me more". Three magic words you can use with every child—tell me more.'

GLOBAL EFFORTS

The global response to the statistics on the emotional well-being and mental health of our children has seen a number of initiatives by governments and educationists. Many of these go back to the basics of meditation, breathing, conflict resolution, and developing empathy and compassion.

For instance, the Australian government has launched the Australian Student Well-being Framework. It's a foundational document that serves as a best practice guide for schools in establishing policies and support mechanisms to improve overall levels of student well-being.

In 2019, a news release from the UK government announced that up to 370 schools would join one of the largest trials in the world to boost the evidence about what works to support mental health and well-being. They would work with mental health experts to learn relaxation techniques, breathing exercises, and other methods to 'Help them regulate their emotions'. The goal of the program is to study which approaches work best for young people in a world of rapid change.[8]

Denmark has consistently ranked in the top three happiest countries in the world in the UN's World Happiness report over the past seven years. The secret to their happiness may stem from their education system and the introduction of mandatory empathy classes, for students aged six to sixteen since 1993. For one hour each week, the children have empathy lessons during 'Klassens tid' or 'The Class's Hour'. Set for a special time once a week, it's a core part of the curriculum, and the purpose is for students to come together in a relaxed and comfortable setting to discuss any problems they may be having. When no issues are raised for discussion, the group comes together and just chills. Through these classes students learn to help their classmates and compete only with themselves. 'It's all about their upbringing. Danish parents raise happy children who grow up to be happy adults who raise happy children and the cycle repeats itself.'[9]

What many people don't realize is that empathy is a learned

---

[8]'One of the largest mental health trials launches in schools', Gov.uk, 4 February 2019.
[9]'In Denmark, Empathy Classes Are Part Of The National Curriculum', *BrightVibes*, 2019.

skill, and that teaching empathy from a young age has not only been proven to make children more emotionally and socially competent, it also greatly reduces bullying and can also help them be more successful as adults in the future.

In 2022, India was ranked 126 in the World Happiness Report by the UN—tenth from the bottom—but some organizations and government are trying to address this.[10] In 2018, the Delhi government launched the Happiness Curriculum. I was curious about this initiative and spoke to Anurag Kundu, chairperson of the Delhi Commission for Protection of Child Rights. He explained that the genesis lay in the reflective nature of the leadership which responded to the levels of stress that they were seeing in students. 'We wanted children to be happier, we wanted children to be reflective, and we wanted children to focus on understanding emotions, and acknowledging emotions. We wanted them to be able to say, "I am sad" and reflect on what's making them sad. How can we let go or take an action on it. So we began to look for organizations, to create the model, the curriculum and the flow.'

Approximately forty teachers, in partnership with four NGOs, were chosen to write a curriculum that would develop 'emotionally sound students'. Before writing the curriculum, the teachers were trained in what is known as 'co-existential thought', which is based on understanding all aspects of life, including spiritual, intellectual, behavioural, and material. According to this philosophy, life satisfaction and happiness can be achieved by being aware of the self, body, family, society, nature, and universe in order to live in harmony.

The non-profit organization Dream a Dream trained the mentor teachers to work with children, using contextualized empathy-based pedagogies and a life-skills approach for children. This philosophy permeates the happiness curriculum to address the learners' emotional and mental needs by creating a stimulating environment through mindfulness, critical thinking, storytelling, and experiential, play-

---

[10]'India ranks very low in World Happiness Report', *The Hindu*, 19 March 2022.

based activities. In the happiness classes, it is not about being right or wrong; it is about allowing students to express themselves, without judgement.

The objectives of this curriculum include developing self-awareness and mindfulness, inculcating skills of critical thinking and inquiry, enabling learners to communicate effectively, and helping learners to apply life skills to deal with stressful and conflicting situations around them. Teachers are not required to finish the syllabus, but rather, to ensure that all children internalize and understand the concepts taught and have the opportunity to participate.[11]

So has it been successful? We don't know yet because they want to let the impact percolate before an assessment is undertaken. 'The system gears itself differently the moment you begin to evaluate it, so we are letting the first three years sow the seeds of change and let it stabilize,' clarifies Anurag. But what they do have is plenty of anecdotal evidence.

Vishal Talreja, co-founder of Dream a Dream, sees the shifts that have taken place. He believes that the relationship between the child and teacher at school has begun to change. A relationship that was earlier based on fear and disengagement has moved to a sense of being a positive relationship. Children now have the confidence to raise their hand and share a viewpoint or, ask a question.

He remembers 'Observing a happiness class and a child put up her hand, and the teacher asked her to share her views, and she had a stammer, the child shared with me that "I have always had a stammer, but earlier I would never speak up because the other girls would laugh at me and I would be very conscious that the teacher would become impatient with me, but now, the teacher gives me space, the other girls don't laugh at me"—that's an indicator of the fundamental shift in the relationships between peers and teachers.'

Clearly, the curriculum appears to have created spaces of safety

---

[11]'Explained: What is Delhi's 'happiness class', and how is it implemented?', *Indian Express*, 23 February 2022.

and empathy in the classroom. The sessions are related to real life and the children are able to apply the stories, the mindful practices, and reflections in their day to day living.

There are marked behavioural changes in the teachers, too, says Vishal. 'The sense of joy and engagement they feel during a happiness class is carried forward through their day to other classes and in their lives at home. Peer relationships amongst teachers have improved, because the stories are having an impact on their own perspectives on life and living, they support each other rather than competing with each other.'

Perhaps the most heartening of all is the systemic change it has brought within the school system. 'It has created a sense of possibility. The school calendar has been sacrosanct for many years, same subjects, same classrooms, it looks the same every year. But by taking five minutes away from other classes and creating a thirty-five minute class, it has opened up teachers' minds to say that if we can bring in something new that is working well in the classroom environment, maybe we can remove something that is not working. Now teachers are exploring what else can we do that is relevant to students today? The Department is now hearing from teachers about new and fresh ideas, new ways of learning, new subjects, how do we look at break time? Teachers have suddenly brought in all their insights and creative energies,' he says with satisfaction.

Vishal is delighted that parents too have welcomed the changes that they see in their children. 'Some mothers have laughingly complained to teachers, "Yeh aapne hamare ladkon ko kar kya rahe ho? Yeh rasoi mein aake madad karta hai"—what are you doing to our sons? They want to come and help in the kitchen now! Clearly he (the child) has reflected on looking at those who do so much for you, and understood that all it takes to show gratitude is to just go up to them and say, "Can I help you?" Children have started to think about things.'

Students are also recognizing a change, especially when it comes to mindfulness activities, such as breathing and stillness and being aware of one's thoughts. One child remarked, 'It makes me feel different…my mind gets refreshed, and it helps me concentrate on the particular subject even if I am not interested.'[12]

And then there are classes that can be labelled a complete disaster. A teacher described a class he observed from the window without anyone knowing he was there. "Aaj hum happiness padhegain, sub log khush ho jao. Husso! Khade ho! Huss kyon nahi rahe ho tum?—And then a smack—Huss ke dekhao!" He shrugged and remarked "Ho gaya happiness class". So it takes all sorts!'

So, how can we raise happy balanced children? How can we hard-wire balance and happiness in the early years? What are the factors that help children be happy and have a strong sense of self and community that builds their emotional well-being? Two factors are important—the outdoors and happier adults. Family activities need to embrace more outdoor activity, connection, and communication and finally what will make your child really happy is knowing that they are the apple of your eye. And that's a truth we have always known!

---

[12]Helyn Kim, Vishal Talreja, and Sreehari Ravindranath, 'How do you measure happiness? Exploring the happiness curriculum in Delhi schools', Brookings Institute, 13 November 2019.

EPILOGUE

Future shock is the shattering stress and disorientation that we induce in individuals by subjecting them to too much change in too short a time.

—Alvin Toffler

Looking back on our journey as parents and educators, I am reminded time and again of the words of Alvin Toffler who coined the term 'future shock'. He refers to what happens to a society when change happens too fast, resulting in social confusion and the breaking down of normal decision-making processes. Accelerated change has defined the last decade. This has been felt in our social structures, family units, institutions, and our relationships; it has led to the redrawing of our value systems and changing our behaviours. We don't feel the shock overnight because change is stealthy and we shift and adapt without realizing we are doing so. It is only when we have the space to reflect and look back that we realize the huge contours of the changes we have experienced, are constantly adjusting to, and the impact it has had.

As a parent and as an educator, all my assumptions have been challenged. I couldn't raise my son the way I had been brought up, my role as a parent was very different from that of my parents and I noted a yawning abyss between my experience and what young parents are experiencing today. Our lives are, in a sense, being driven by commercialization, consumerism, digitalization, and the apparent erosion of our held beliefs. These changes, like the pandemic, have changed the way we live, learn, and work and the way we communicate. In short, it has impacted our relationships. So the question we struggle with is—how do we navigate this?

I was struck by the title of a book which stared at me from a six-foot-high poster at the Rupa/Aleph office. *What the Heck Do I Do with My Life?*—a question I have been asked by thousands of students particularly over the last decade. Author Ravi Venkatesan's tag line offers hopeful solutions on 'how to flourish in our turbulent times'. He poses the question that besets us: What do I do with my life? In my conversations with young people, this comes up as the foremost point of their anxiety as they live in uncertain times, unable to predict which way the world will turn next. Will they be able to go to university? Will they find jobs? Will their lives ever be the same again?

According to Venkatesan, our children and grandchildren are inhabiting a VUCA Universe. (Yet another acronym for us to embrace!) VUCA stands for volatility, uncertainty, complexity, and ambiguity. It describes the situation of constant and unpredictable change that is now the norm in certain industries and areas of the business world.[1]

The volatility, uncertainty, complexity, and ambiguity of the future is closing in on young adults in their final years at school. What follows is a series of poignant and mature responses to my question to groups of teenagers about how they see the future, and how it made them feel.

'Very scary. Just the fact that you can't really plan for it. You can make a framework that could get so messed up overnight by things you cannot foresee. I don't know what's going to happen—you have no control. Currently the pressure of right wing terror that has swept the world scares me'.

'I'm mixed up. I am looking forward to getting away to another continent without parental pressure and lots of independence. But it's also scary.'

---

[1]Ravi Venkatesan, *What The Heck Do I Do With My Life? How To Flourish In Our Turbulent Times*, New Delhi: Rupa Publications India, 2021.

'The instability of the world around me genuinely frightens me. I have huge anxiety about not being able to trust people. So I put my worst foot forward—doubting, forbidding, closed—but I found that there were friends and family who still chose to support me. I now know that I can always fall back on these people who won't judge you, who will listen to your fears, and see that they are valid, and work on them with you.'

'I am so fearful and uncertain about the future. As schools shut down, board exams were in limbo, college admissions appeared unrealistic, it was a time of confusion, and I kept asking questions which no one could answer—What will happen next? Where do we go from here?'

'I feel as if I have no control. I lost that sense of security and structure I was used to feeling with my family. Particularly during the pandemic second wave, for the first time in my life, I saw people I knew getting Covid, and when I experienced what it can do to your loved ones, the gravity of the situation slapped me in the face. It leaves you feeling desolate and worried. It left me confused. I couldn't understand why, in spite of our developed technology, people were dying. I struggle to come to grips with that. It left me wondering whether things will ever be alright again.'

'The scale of loss and death was an experience that many had never experienced. I cannot think of a day in that month when we didn't wake up to bad news. Thirty days and we had heard of thirty deaths in our colony, of our family and friends. I asked my mother and grandfather, "Has something like this ever happened to you before?" My grandfather said, in his eighty-plus years of living, they haven't woken up to news of death every morning. "It feels like war to us."'

'It is a rollercoaster, mentally, physically, in every which way. I am left hanging, wondering whether I can go forward in anyway. I feel mentally drained. I don't know what is right for me. I don't have the comfort of knowing what the future holds. I am stuck. Right now I have no hope. I wish someone would make the decisions for me, and help me take control of my life.'

'Everything seems to be irrelevant, even the course I am studying doesn't seem to matter any more. I can't seem to think clearly, to prioritize, because the uncertainty is always present.'

Others felt they had to let go. They had to learn to take every day as it comes because no one knew what tomorrow would bring. According to Ravi the only way to deal with VUCA is to live with 'Intentionality and be anchored in your beliefs, purposes, commitments, and core relationships'. And that of course means knowing what they are and becoming as he says 'Intentional about your life'. He makes a strong case for us to view ourselves as 'spiritual beings' able to control our minds and our reactions, and realizing the connectedness between us as human beings and the environment.

There are reverberations of the tenets of practically all faiths in his statement, for instance, Buddhism speaks of interdependence and 'dependent arising', as does the philosophy of Vedanta. Even as mounting challenges have made life increasingly difficult for children, especially during the pandemic, our individualistic and materialistic cultures have only led to more isolation. So, how can we address the uncertainty that looms large in young minds? Marian de Souza writes how 'A child is a "multi-dimensional being; an individual with a rational mind that thinks, an emotional mind that feels and a spiritual mind that intuits, imagines, wonders and creates"'.[2] The pandemic exposed a world beset with economic and social disparity. In such a world, spirituality can teach children to reflect on their actions and the world, perform acts of kindness, and comfort others and themselves. Not to be confused with religion and morality, 'Spiritual development is the process of growing the intrinsic human capacity for self-transcendence, in which the self is embedded in something greater than itself, including the sacred. It is the developmental "engine" that propels the search for connectedness, meaning, purpose,

---

[2]Marian de Souza, 'The Spiritual Dimension of Education in Addressing Issues of Identity and Belonging', *Discourse and Communication for Sustainable Education*, 2016.

and contribution. It is shaped both within and outside of religious traditions, beliefs, and practices.'[3]

So can we pop a spiritual pill which makes a huge difference straight away? Not so easily. First, we have to stop depending on a particular set of circumstances to make us happy, such as, we must be in good health, be young, handsome and beautiful, successful, rich and popular, with lots of Instagram likes. These are impossible parameters for happiness. Because ours is a world of change, it takes very little to make us unhappy and it takes a lot to make us happy. We cannot go into the world with a begging bowl asking for happiness. Once we recognize that the nature of this world is such that we cannot have everlasting happiness, we understand that spiritual pursuit brings us the daily benefits of reflection, meditation and service—the benefits are of peace, meaningful existence, and being a blessing to others.

As adults we may have evolved enough to consider the above as a way of life. Personally, I began to reflect on these eternal questions only when I hit my mid-fifties, but in all the decades prior to this insight, I was hopelessly engaged in a tussle for happiness that would elude me. And for young people in their teens, they have a long way to go before they start to internalize this philosophy. But given the concerns around the emotional well-being and mental health of our children, there have been a number of global initiatives by governments and educationists. Many of these go back to the basics of meditation, breathing, conflict resolution, and developing empathy and compassion. No doubt these will help them get on to the path of reflection and understanding that their happiness lies within.

But unless similar shifts take place within us, parents and educators, our children will find little support in their efforts. We have to shift our expectations, change our perspectives and look within our own lives as adults and I truly believe that this void needs to be addressed

---

[3]Vicki Zakrzewski, 'The Case for Discussing Spirituality in Schools', *Greater Good Magazine*, 8 January 2013.

if we want our children's futures to be more anchored and stable in complex and changing times.

I wondered, where does hope lie when we are filled with so much uncertainty and unhappiness within ourselves? I put this question to a number of specialists and therapists who have been working with parents and children in the hope of getting a ray of light about what the future holds and how we could hold on to a sense of hope.

Gloria Burrett was thoughtful in her response, almost waiting for the answer to emerge. After a few minutes, she defined in her gentle manner that for her, hope lies 'In the shape of an adult who dares to really honour that call of being the wise elder, the wise respectful elder. Any opportunity for connection and conversation, equal respect for all—this for me brings hope.' This is a call for adults, both parents and educators, to deeply introspect on the need to be 'present' for their children, to make deep connections with them through dialogue and conversation. It is difficult, because as adults we carry our share of anxieties and stresses both personally and professionally, and indeed in our own ways are stumbling through a VUCA Universe.

Connection and conversation—two words that have continued to reverberate through my discussions with children and parents over the last three years! As a parent, it is tough to be resilient in the face of your recalcitrant adolescent who refuses to let you in. How do you start? Where do you begin? Dr Shelja Sen looks at this problem from the lens of the popular phrase—'It takes a community to raise a child'! She believes that these conversations must take place in schools which for her 'is the most beautiful place for all this to happen. Think on it. It's a readymade community that parents, teachers, and children are a part of and which allows these conversations to take place. How can we not become aware of the level of the problems of fear, anxiety, and a fractured sense of self that our children and we are facing? It's not something that one school counsellor can tackle. All those working with children need to say, "Let's get together and do something about it." Rajani, counsellor at St Mary's School too, believes that 'Having designated counsellors is not the answer. It is only when parents, teachers and children are jointly involved in talking about the stresses we face that we can hope for positive outcomes.'

Janani Iyer has spent a lot of time introspecting and believes parents and educators need to work on themselves, own their story and not get caught up in what she calls the 'shame web' if they want to help their children. 'You're indestructible if you own it. I battled depression in 2008 and I started talking about it to my class ten kids, because I knew I had a student who was struggling with it too. I told him, I know how you're feeling. There are certain days when you get up feeling that way. Then you have to tell yourself, "Okay, I am going to get up, I'll probably listen to this particular song that peps me up", and suddenly it becomes like a very easy conversation because you're ready to own it.'

For an adult this is not easy. It calls for being in touch with who you are as a person and owning your own vulnerability, and that, says Shania, a counsellor at the Shri Ram School, is critical. 'Owning vulnerability opens you up in different ways. Because beyond my role as educator, therapist, whatever, we are all human beings, and I see everyone as human. Each one of us has a story which is unique in its own way and it is important for your story to have an audience. Like Rumi would say—"You're not a drop in the ocean, you're the entire ocean"—let it flow. Shit happens, for students, for teachers, for parents, you're going to go through that, we all learn on the job. As a therapist, I have become a better therapist because I am very much in touch with who I am as a person.'

It calls for dropping your defences and accepting that we are only human and we will make mistakes, both as parents and educators, as we journey through the ups and downs of raising our children. And very often the answers come from the children. I gained a great deal of insight from an ex-student who smiled and said we have to shed the myth of happy families. 'Families have to be human—parents make mistakes, children make mistakes. Parents must try not to have a perception of what they want their child to be. When a child is born they have so many dreams and aspirations for this child and they want the child to be happy and successful. As a parent, somewhere along the line you also have to look at what they are, and not how you want them to be. As parents you can't completely know, and that's alright too.'

As parents many of us want to be the ideal mother or father, with the ideal set of children, and believe that happiness begins with external markers—good marks, success, wealth, fame, and fortune. But as wisdom tells us happiness lies within. And very few of us spend that time working on our inner selves, working on our empathy, compassion, and kindness.

As Dr Shelja Sen believes, our hope is our children. 'I am hopeful because young people give me hope, that's why I like working with young people. On one hand there's a sense of despair when I work with them. Their sense of life being meaningless is so strong sometimes. Yet on the other hand, they come up with ideas, they're more open, and I've seen young teachers are open to ideas and I also feel, like you're talking about it, and you're writing a book about it, if we have more and more people having these conversations about it and not just locate the problem in the child and the family and start seeing it in a larger context with larger conversations, I do think a change can happen.'

The conversations with the students began in 2018, and by 2021, I felt it was time to bring together all the students whom I had spoken to at length, to understand how they were navigating a VUCA world. What had held them through this time? How had they changed? What had they learned?

Their resilience, determination, and courage gave me so much hope for all of us! Some found a discipline within themselves that they never thought they had. Jayant felt that he finally took charge by telling himself 'Because the world is in disarray, it is not an excuse to let go of myself. I put in effort and determination—it was like a turning point when I decided to make the best of the present moment.' He pushed himself into a tough fitness regimen, rediscovered his love for reading, and realized that he loves fantasy because, 'Entering other worlds gave me a sense of optimism. In these worlds people are battling dark, evil forces, and coming out triumphant, that gives me hope. The same will inevitably happen for us. It was a 100 per cent escape.'

For all of them, communication, connection, the love and support from friends and family was what held them together. For Anaya it was her family, 'My parents were like rocks, they were unfazed while everything was falling around us. That was so very comforting and our really good friends got us through somehow, through extended phone calls and just being available any time of day or night.'

Many rediscovered and cemented family relationships—for Jasmine, it was getting to know her family again! 'You don't get this type of time when everything is at a standstill and you're forced to interact with each other, and acknowledge each other. So we're playing board games and watching movies, at times getting on each other's nerves, there's a lot of yelling and fighting, but we're connected and communicating. I've learned to be more sensitive to people around me, and to see them as more human. To acknowledge that they're not perfect, we all have our faults and weaknesses and we began to be sensitive to what we were all going through."

Praveen began to appreciate the small things. 'I began to appreciate nature, the outdoors, running, and being able to go out for a coffee, you realize the value of little things that you take for granted. I have begun to appreciate all I have.' And that was echoed by Ravi, 'I've learned to appreciate the people who have been there for me. I don't like to talk about my emotions, but I've learned to appreciate people's kindness.'

Our hope and the future lies in the hands of all the young people whose voices I have heard during my last three decades in education and through my journey of writing the book. As an educator, I have watched them rise and confront their fears of a world that will remain fractured through their lifetimes. They have looked within and found the empathy and compassion to respond to the needs of those around them. They have learnt the lessons of living in the present, appreciating the unfolding moment, and treasuring their loved ones, friends, and family.

A sense of early maturity has been forced upon our young. They have had to make the best of every situation. They have learned to let go, to stop reacting to the onslaught on social media, videos, petitions, and accept that that there are so many things they cannot control and as Anaya quietly put it, 'At the end of the day, the picture is not yours to predict'. Words of wisdom and profundity from an eighteen-year-old.

They are doing their best to navigate with strength, reflecting a resilient maturity, and critically, an appreciation of being able to live in the present moment whilst being empathetic, compassionate, and above all, full of gratitude. Jayant captured this with precision and sincerity, 'I now know that if things do not go your way, it is possible to see the light and reach the light at the end of the tunnel. I also learned a vital lesson—cherish things that are important to you like your family, time, memories, experience, conversations, a walk on the terrace, staring at a mango tree from the window together, I got a better sense of gratitude.'

Writing in *The Week*, Navtej Sarna eloquently and poignantly voiced this shift in our young people. 'This will be the summer when the generation to which my children belong suddenly grew up. They started using their phones not for posting photographs of what they were eating and drinking but to help find oxygen cylinders or hospital beds or life-saving drugs for friends. Hospitals, ICUs, crematoria, and virtual condolence meetings entered their carefree lexicon and death was no longer something that happened only to grandparents. They learnt, too, the value of doing good in however small a measure. They realized, earlier in life than usual, the emptiness of material success and observed in impotent rage that wealth mostly meets only selfish ends. They learnt the limited reach of good intentions and the sickening helplessness of hitting your head against a wall. Their belief that a modern world will only get better has been proven false.'[4]

In closing, I wanted to share two personal reflections which were triggered by Sarna's impassioned passage. The first was when I lost my husband to cancer in 2020, which came out of nowhere and left us dazed and numb as we dealt with our loss. Bill was a teacher and a football coach during the thirty years he spent in India. I didn't realize the warmth and depth of his relationships with the students who were scattered across the world until the word that he was gone spread, and messages came pouring in. These were once children who had spent time with him on the football field and at camps, and were now adults heading various vectors globally—but they reached out. They reached out to me with love and warmth and wrote about him with empathy, his crazy sense of humour, steely grit, tough love, relentless determination, and, most importantly, an unwavering commitment to all his students. Each message was different. Each had been difficult to write. Each was personal. I have them all, as precious memories, and I cannot thank them enough for sharing them with so much compassion—and for making the time to do so.

The second instance was when a much loved teacher and head of a physical education department lost his struggle to Covid. His family and friends were in shock. Noriyal sir was a man of the mountains, an excellent mountaineer and athlete, gentle, kind, with the patience of a saint, and was always fit as a fiddle. For the students whom he had trained, counselled, encouraged, and comforted when the chips were down, he was a legend. An appeal was launched by the students of the schools he was associated with and a crowd sourcing fund was initiated for his family. All of this came from students, from young people, and within the first twenty-four hours, the funding target was not just achieved, it was doubled. I was so moved to learn that the contributions were coming in currencies from across the globe,

---

[4]Navtej Sarna, 'Time lost and opportunities missed do not come back, writes Navtej Sarna', *The Week*, 13 June 2021.

and more importantly, the tributes his students paid him were a testimony to how well they knew him, they remembered his qualities of affection, kindness, strong integrity, fair play, sportsmanship, and honour. They articulated their feelings with a warmth that many adults would find hard to do.

So, despite all the challenges of a dystopian present, I have hope; I am seeing many young people emerge rooted, stronger, and with sound personal values. I have faith in our young. And I can sense that this centeredness is down to balanced parenting and school support.

Children need the security that unconditional love gives them. Families and teachers can be the buffers against the uncertainties of their lives. Our anxieties rub off on them at every stage, and as parents and educators we have to set them aside, work on ourselves first, so we are that 'wise elder' that is there for them, nurturing their security. This gives them the inner confidence to know they can overcome problems. Most importantly we need to be 'present'. Supportive and loving relationships are at the core of their sense of self, and their sense of optimism. In their resilience lies our hope.

Had I the heavens' embroidered cloths,
Enwrought with golden and silver light,
The blue and the dim and the dark cloths
Of night and light and the half light,
I would spread the cloths under your feet:
But I, being poor, have only my dreams;
I have spread my dreams under your feet;
Tread softly because you tread on my dreams.

—W. B. Yeats

ACKNOWLEDGEMENTS

The last few years have been a challenging time for humanity as a whole. The deeply personal loss of my husband, Bill, in the midst of the pandemic, brought me close to putting my writing in the bottom drawer. I owe this book to my editor Pujitha Krishnan who was my lighthouse, navigator, and coach all rolled into one. Her guidance was always clear and gentle and she gave me confidence at a time when I needed it most. I must add my thanks and gratitude to my copy editor Karishma Koshal, who brought precision, reflection, and questioning to the work, and to Aleph Book Company for this opportunity which has been a journey of learning.

When I began writing four years ago, I was sure about one thing—the book needed to reflect the voices of parents, students, and educators. And as I began to connect with networks of these communities I was overwhelmed by their generous response. We met in focused group discussions, in schools, at One Up Library, in coffee shops, at my home around my dining table, and when the pandemic rolled on, through Zoom and on video calls across the globe. Their voices shaped and structured the narrative that began to emerge. To each and every individual who trusted me with their challenges, their experiences of pain and revelation, I owe an enormous debt of gratitude, thank you!

I am very grateful to the child psychologists and counsellors who gave me so much of their precious time. My warm thanks to Dr Shelja Sen, Gloria Burrett, Carol Paul, Rajani Khanduja, Shania, Janani Iyer, and Sonal Ahuja, whose perspectives were insightful, and their commitment to their work, inspirational.. Special thanks to the educators Dr Annie Koshy, Manika Sharma, Dr Sonya Philips,

Kiran Tara Singh, Pooja Jain, Namritha Rathee, Dr Sonal Parmar, Madhumita Ramakrishnan, Gita Dang, Meena Cariappa, Shalloo Sharma, Vishal Talreja, and Anurag Kundu for sharing the challenges of nurturing children and supporting parents in our complex and anxious times.

Writing is a lonely effort. And yet with the wealth of conversations that I had, the reflections that were triggered about my own life as a parent and educator have been enriching. As parents, if there was a memo we received from their stories, it is that of loving, letting go, and always being there for our children. I hope I have done their narratives justice.

The support, guidance, and generosity of family and friends has held me through this journey. For over forty years, Bill had been my strongest ally and severest critic, and that mantle has been passed to my son who has encouraged me at every step to complete this endeavour, and for that I am deeply grateful.

RECOMMENDED READING

Alexander, Jessican Joelle and Sandahl, Iben Dissing, *The Danish Way of Parenting*, New York: TarcherPerigee, 2016.

Blakemore, Sarah-Jayne, *Inventing Ourselves: The Secret Life of the Teenage Brain*, New York: Public Affairs, 2018.

Cariappa, Meena and Dang, Gita, *Meeting Early Challenges: Special Steps for a Special Child*, Lucknow: UBS Publishers, 2005.

Esquith, Rafa, *Teach Like Your Hair's on Fire*, New York: Penguin Viking, 2007.

Faber, Adele and Mazlish, Elaine, *How to Talk So Kids Will Listen & Listen So Kids Will Talk*, New York: Scribner, 2012.

Fosslien, Liz and Duffy, Molly West, *No Hard Feelings: Emotions at Work and How They Help Us Succeed*, New York: Penguin Random House, 2019.

Gibran, Kahlil, *The Prophet*, New York: Alfred A Knopf, 1973.

Ginott, Haim, *Between Parent & Teenager*, New York: Avon Books, 1985.

——, *Between Parent & Child*, New York: Three Rivers Press, 2003.

——, *Teacher & Child*, New York: Macmillan, 1972.

Gray, Peter, *Free to Learn: Why Unleashing the Instinct to Play Will Make Our Children Happier, More Self-Reliant, and Better Students for Life*, New York: Basic Books, 2013.

Gupta, Aditi and Paul, Tuhin, *Menstrupedia: The Friendly Guide To Periods For Girls*, New Delhi: Menstrupedia, 2016.

Hobson, Tom, *Teacher Tom's First Book: Teaching and Learning from Preschoolers*, Seattle: Peanut Butter Publishing, 2017.

Holt, John, *How Children Learn*, Lebanon: Da Capo Press, 2017.

Lemov, Doug, *Teach Like A Champion*, Hoboken: Jossey-Bass, 2015.

Levine, Madeline, *The Price of Privilege: How Parental Pressure and Material Advantage Are Creating a Generation of Disconnected and Unhappy Kids*, New York: Harper Collins, 2006.

Malkan, Stacy, *Not Just a Pretty Face: The Ugly Side of the Beauty Industry*, Gabriola Island: New Society Publishers, 2007.

Mukunda, Kamal V., *What Did You Ask at School Today?*, New Delhi: Harper Collins, 2018.

Nagel, Gretel, *The Tao of Teaching*, New York: Plume Publishing, 1998.

Sen, Shelja, *All you Need is Love: The Art of Mindful Parenting*, New Delhi: Harper Collins India, 2015.

——, *Imagine: No Child Left Invisible*, New Delhi: Harper Collins India, 2017.

——, *Reclaim Your Life*, New Delhi: Westland Publications, 2018.

Tapscott, Don, *Grown Up Digital: The Rise of the Net Generation*, New York: McGraw Hill Education, 2009.

Turkle, Sherry, *Reclaiming Conversation: The Power of Talk in a Digital Age*, Penguin Books, 2016.

Venkatesan, Ravi, *What the Heck Do I Do with My Life? How to Flourish in Our Turbulent Times*, New Delhi: Rupa Publications, 2022.

William, James, *Stand Out of Our Light: Freedom and Resistance in the Attention Economy*, Cambridge: Cambridge University Press, 2018.

Wolf, Maryanne, *Reader Come Home: The Reading Brain in a Digital World*, New Delhi: HarperCollins, 2018.

INDEX

consumer culture, 21–26
consumer driven society, ix, 12
Continuous Partial Attention, 64
Cosmopolitan, 71
Covid-19 pandemic, xii, xv, 3, 8,
    11–12, 17, 65, 183, 193, 147,
    149, 168, 185–86
cyberbullying, 60, 69–70, 100–
    102, 113

Dalwai, Samir, 22
de Souza, Marian, 186
Delhi Commission for the
    Protection of Child Rights,
    134, 179
dendrites development between
    (0–5 years) age, 29
depression, xii, xiii, xv, 46, 80,
    102, 104, 107–108, 134,
    150–53, 155, 161, 171, 189
digital families, 26–31
digitalization of lives, viii, xii, 58,
    183
discipline, 24–26, 71, 167, 190
domestic violence, 161
Dr Seuss (books), 31
Dream a Dream organization,
    179–80

early maturity among children, 45
Electronic Screen Syndrome, 60
elite privileged schools, pressure
    on middle-class parents, 57–58

Fear of Missing Out (FOMO),
    81, 96
Federation of Obstetrics and

Gynaecologists Society of India
    (FOGSI)
    survey on girls sexual maturity
    in urban India, 45
Fosslien, Liz and Duffy, Mollie
    West
    *No Hard Feelings: Emotions at
    Work and How They Help Us
    Succeed,* 142, 142n6
French, Christine, 34

Gates, Melinda, 30
Gay-Related Infectious Disease
    (GRID), 116
generational gap, ix, xi
GenZ, 80
Gibran, Kahlil, 2
Ginott, Haim
    Between Parent & Teenager and
    *Teacher & Child The Common
    Sense Book of Baby and Child
    Care,* vii
Glancy, Josh, 95
    on Instagrammability, 96
Graham, Richard, 59
Gray, Peter, 9n1
    Free to Learn, 9

Happiness Curriculum of Delhi
    Government, 179–82
Herman-Giddens, Marcia, 46
Hobson, Tom
    *Teacher Tom's First Book:
    Teaching and Learning from
    Preschoolers,* 10
hormonal changes, 45
Huffington Post, 35

Hygen, Beate Wold, 67
hyperventilating, 104

independent adults, 77
Indian Academy of Pediatrics
(IAP), 22
*International Journal of Preventive
Medicine,* 28–29
internet use among children,
guidelines for, 59–60
IVF process, 5
Iyer, Janani, 50, 164, 169,
171–172, 174–77, 189

Jain, Pooja, 44, 47, 55–56, 63
Jobs, Steve, 30
journal(s)
Developmental Psychology, 19
*Journal of Development &
Behavioral Pediatrics,* 36
Pediatrics, 9–10, 22

Keeley, Paul, 78
Khanduja, Rajani, 50, 156
Kids Growing Older Younger
Faster (KGOYF) phenomenon,
x, 44, 152–53
Krsitakis, Erika, 64
Kundu, Anurag, 134–35, 179

Levine, Madeline, 18, 18n5
*The Price of Privilege: How
Parental Pressure and Material
Advantage Are Creating a
Generation of Disconnected and
Unhappy Kids,* 51, 74n28, 76
LGBTQ community, 118–21

Section 377, judgement on,
119–20, 159

MacColl, Ewan, 1
Malkan, Stacy
*Not Just a Pretty Face: The Ugly
Side of the Beauty Industry,* 56
Maurer, Uwe, 127
*Meeting Early Challenges: Special
Steps for a Special Child* (Meena
Cariappa and Gita Dang),
128–132
Menstrupedia (Aditi Gupta and
Tuhin Paul), 48–49
mental health of children
and role of teachers, 168–71
behavioural disorder, 150
changing landscape, 150–167
classroom communities through
Circle Time power, 171–77
communication disorder, 150
global response to emotional
well-being and, 177–82
learning disabilities, 150
mental disorders among
children and adolescents, 149
Mirchandani, Dayal, 60–61
mobile phone in India, children
users, 28
mobile technology use by parents
and young children, 31–33
moral codes, importance of
discussion and dialogues for,
102, 111, 126
multi-dimensional being of child,
186

Stand Out of Our Light, 30–31

World Economic Forum, xv

World Health Organization, 31
   India as most depressed country
      in world, 149
   report on anxiety disorders, 150

Yeats, W. B., 194

youth culture, 22

Zuckerberg, Mark, 31